WRINKLIES'
PUZZLES

This is a Prion Book.
This edition published in 2010 by Prion
An imprint of the Carlton Publishing Group
20 Mortimer Street
London W1T 3JW

A CIP catalogue for this book is available from the British Library.

ISBN 978 1 85375 775 4

Printed in the UK by CPI Mackays, Chatham, ME5 8TD

WRINKLIES' PUZZLES

Clever Conundrums for Older Intellects

PRION

CONTENTS

INTRODUCTION

Welcome to this book of puzzles, designed just for you
– the happy-go-lucky, freedom-loving wrinkly. Now you
already know that a big part of youth is stored in the
brain. "You're as old as you feel", and all that. But it's also
true that as one matures (yes, I mean you're getting a bit
older) one needs to ensure sure that the brain gets regular
exercise – just as with your body. Luckily for all of us,
brain exercise can be done from the comfort of a favourite
armchair. That's where this book comes in. Do a few
puzzles a day and keep your grey matter in great shape! As
well as the wide variety of puzzles inside, we've included
some funny, uplifting and downright silly quotations for
you too, so you won't get bored.

Enjoy the book, and keep yourself young!

EASY
PUZZLES

BITS AND PIECES: How can you mend a
broken heart? Here's four you can practise on. Match each half heart
with its partner to make four whole ones.

Answer on page 156

BOXES: Playing the game of boxes, each player takes it in
turns to join two adjacent dots with a line. If a player's line completes
a box, the player wins the box and has another go. It's your turn in the
game below. To avoid giving your opponent a lot of boxes, what's your
best move?

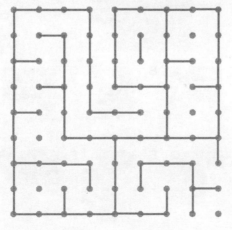

Answer on page 156

CUT AND FOLD: Which of the patterns below is created by this fold and cut?

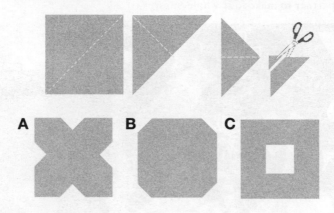

A **B** **C**

Answer on page 156

GAME OF TWO HALVES: Which two shapes below will pair up to create the top shape?

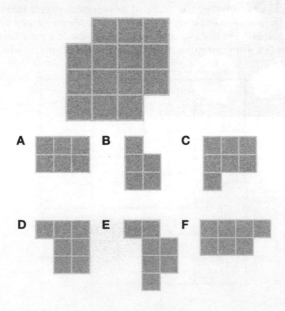

A **B** **C**

D **E** **F**

Answer on page 156

DOUBLE DRAT: All these shapes appear twice in the box except one. Can you spot the singleton?

Answer on page 156

9

IN THE AREA: Can you work out the approximate area that this dog is taking up?

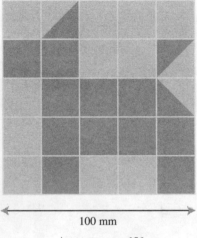

100 mm

Answer on page 156

JIGSAW: Which three of the pieces below can complete the jigsaw and make a perfect square?

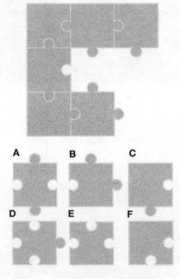

A **B** **C**

D **E** **F**

Answer on page 156

SUM PEOPLE: Work out what number is represented by which person and replace the question mark.

1 32

2 4 3

1 4 1

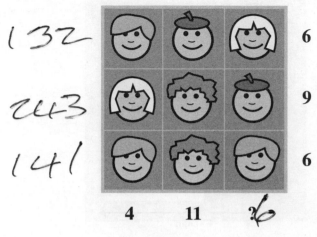

6

9

6

4   11   ?6

Answer on page 156

SHAPE SHIFTING: Fill in the empty squares so that each row, column and long diagonal contains five different symbols

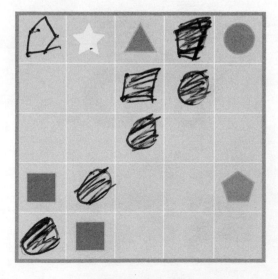

Answer on page 156

POTS OF DOTS: How many dots should there be in the hole in this pattern?

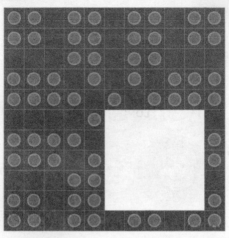

Answer on page 157

PICTURE PARTS: Which box has exactly the right bits to make the pic?

A **B** **C**

Answer on page 157

ODD CLOCKS: Buenos Aires is 11 hours behind

Singapore, which is 7 hours ahead of London. It is 6.55 pm on Tuesday in London – what time is it in the other two cities?

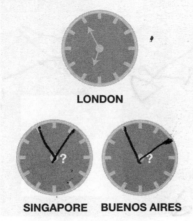

LONDON

SINGAPORE   BUENOS AIRES

Answer on page 157

MASYU: Draw a single continuous line around the grid that passes

through all the circles. The line must enter and leave each box in the centre of one of its four sides. **Black Circle:** Turn left or right in the box, and the line must pass straight through the next and previous boxes.

White Circle: Travel straight through the box, and the line must turn in the next and/or previous box.

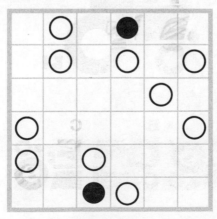

Answer on page 157

MATRIX: Which of the boxed figures completes the set?

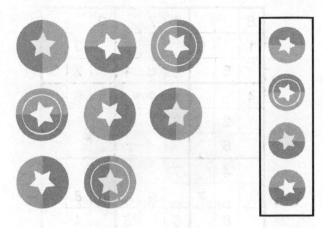

Answer on page 157

FACE IN THE CROWD: Can you find one
face in the crowd that isn't quite as happy as all the others?

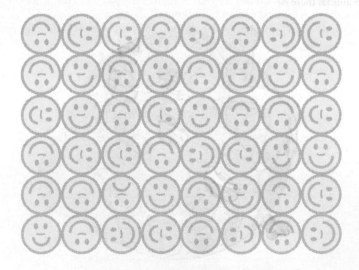

Answer on page 157

SUDOKU: Complete the grid so that all rows and columns, and each outlined block of nine squares, contain the numbers 1, 2, 3, 4, 5, 6, 7, 8 and 9.

8			1	7		2		
1		9			6		3	
	5			3	4		7	8
4			8	2		5	9	
	2		3		9		1	
	6							3
	4		7					2
		7		4	2	6	8	
	8		6		3		4	

Answer on page 157

RIDDLE: An enclosure at the zoo contains both elephants and emus. If there are a total of 44 feet and 30 eyes, can you work out how many of each animal there is?

Answer on page 157

15

BITS AND PIECES: Can you match the four broken tops of these vases with the bodies they belong to?

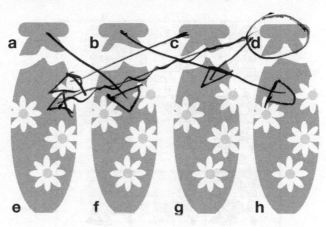

Answer on page 158

CUT AND FOLD: Which of the patterns below is created by this fold and cut?

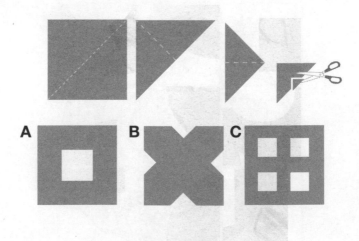

Answer on page 158

MIRROR IMAGE: Only one of these pictures is an exact mirror image of the first one? Can you spot it?

Answer on page 158

NUMBER JIGSAW: The nine boxes that make up this grid can be rearranged to make a number. Which number?

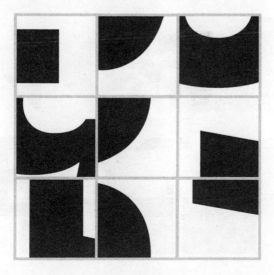

Answer on page 158

MISSING LINK: What should replace the square with the question mark so that the grid follows a pattern?

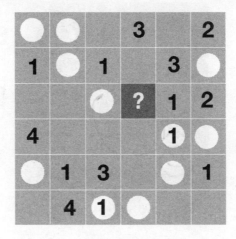

Answer on page 158

PICTURE PARTS: Which box has exactly the right bits to make the pic?

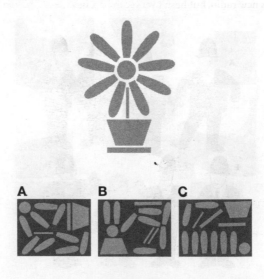

A   **B**   **C**

Answer on page 158

SUM PEOPLE: Work out what number is represented by which person and replace the question mark.

8

8

11

8   *10*?   9

Answer on page 158

USUAL SUSPECTS: Officer Lassiter is having his new uniform and kit fitted. He has the helmet badge, but not the shoulder badges yet. He has his new radio, but hasn't yet received a new tie... Can you pick him out of the group?

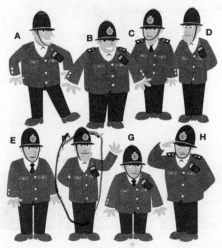

Answer on page 158

WHERE'S THE PAIR?: Only two of these
pictures are exactly the same. Can you spot the matching pair?

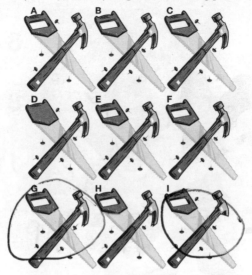

Answer on page 158

ODD CLOCKS: Madrid is 7 hours behind Tokyo, which
is 1 hour behind Melbourne. It is 6.15 am on Saturday in Tokyo – what time is it
in the other two cities?

TOKYO

MELBOURNE   **MADRID**

Answer on page 158

WHERE'S THE PAIR?: Only two of the shapes
below are exactly the same – can you find the matching pair?

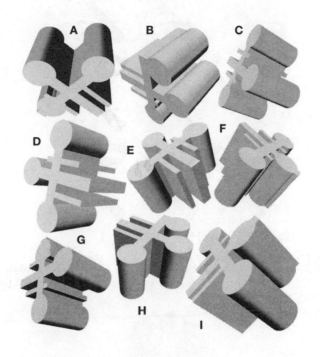

Answer on page 158

WHERE'S THE PAIR: Only two of these
pictures are exactly the same. Can you spot the matching pair?

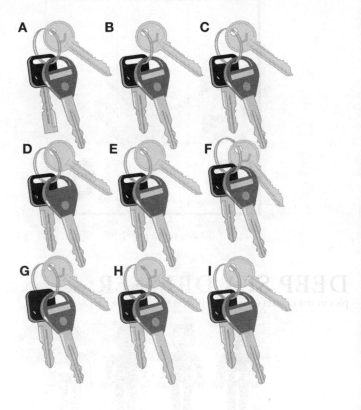

Answer on page 159

MAGIC SQUARES: Complete the square using nine consecutive numbers, so that all rows, columns and large diagonals add up to the same total.

Answer on page 159

DEEP SEA DRESSER: Arrange this set of diver pics in the correct order from boxers to ocean-prepared.

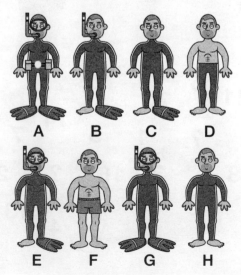

A B C D

E F G H

Answer on page 159

GAME OF TWO HALVES: Which two
shapes below will pair up to create the top shape?

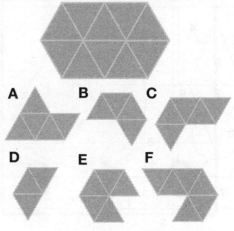

Answer on page 159

HUB SIGNS: What numbers should appear in the hubs of
these number wheels?

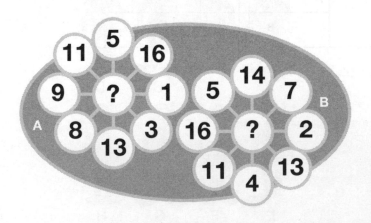

Answer on page 159

PAINT BY NUMBERS: Colour in the odd
numbers to reveal... What?

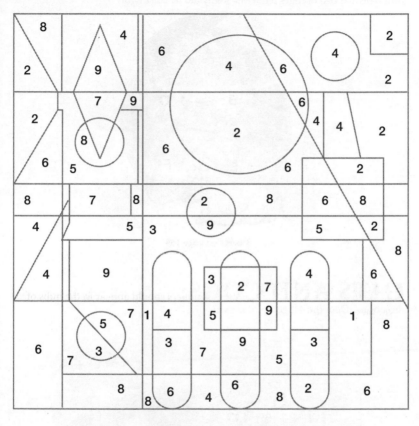

Answer on page 159

25

RIDDLE: Billy bought a bag of oranges on Monday and ate a third of them. On Tuesday he ate half of the oranges he had left. On Wednesday he found he had two oranges left. How many did he start with?

Answer on page 159

CATS AND COGS: Turn the handle in the indicated direction... Does the cat go up or down?

Answer on page 159

CHECKERS: Make a move for white so that eight black pieces are left, none which are in the same column or row.

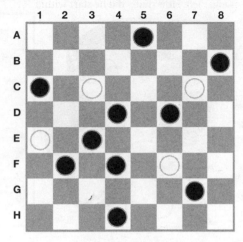

Answer on page 159

IN THE AREA: Can you work out the approximate area this bird is taking up?

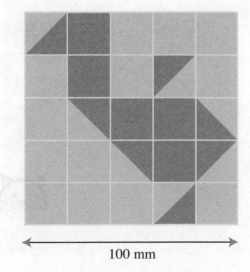

100 mm

Answer on page 159

MATRIX: Which of the boxed figures completes the set?

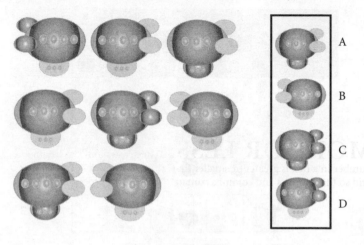

Answer on page 160

MISSING LINK: What should replace the square with the question mark so that the grid follows a pattern?

Answer on page 160

SUM TOTAL: Replace the question marks with
mathematical symbols (+,−, × or ÷) to make a working sum.

$$16 \; ? \; 2 \; ? \; 3 \; ? \; 1 = 6$$

Answer on page 160

MORE OR LESS: The arrows indicate whether a
number in a box is greater or smaller than an adjacent number. Complete the
grid so that all rows and columns contain the numbers 1 to 5.

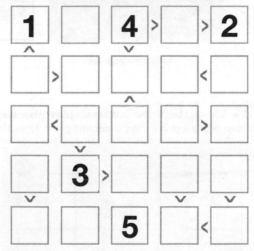

Answer on page 160

29

RIDDLE:

It's night time in your bedroom and the light has broken. You're getting dressed and need a pair of socks. You've got 10 red, 8 white and 12 grey socks in a drawer – how many do you have to pull out in the dark before you know you have a matching pair?

Answer on page 160

BOXES:

Playing the game of boxes, each player takes it in turns to join two adjacent dots with a line. If a player's line completes a box, the player wins the box and has another go. It's your turn in the game below. To avoid giving your opponent a lot of boxes, what's your best move?

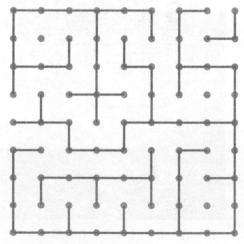

Answer on page 160

DOUBLE DRAT: All these numbers appear twice in the box except one. Can you spot the singleton?

Answer on page 161

BOATS AND BUOYS: Every buoy 🔵 has one boat ⬭ found horizontally or vertically adjacent to it. No boat can be in an adjacent square to another boat (even diagonally). The numbers by each row and column tell you how many boats there are. Can you locate all the boats?

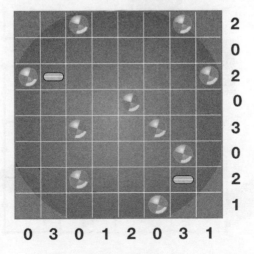

Answer on page 161

RIDDLE:

Tony and Tina go shopping and on the way home Tina says, "Hey! If you gave me one of your bags, I'd have twice as many as you – but if I gave you one of mine, we'd have the same number!" Can you work out how many bags they each have?

Answer on page 161

CUBISM:

The shape below can be folded to make a cube. Which of the four cubes pictured below could it make?

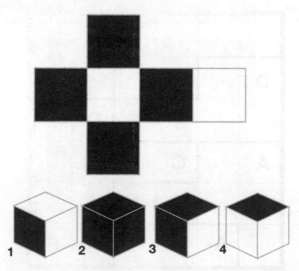

Answer on page 161

CUT AND FOLD: Which of the patterns below is created by this fold and cut?

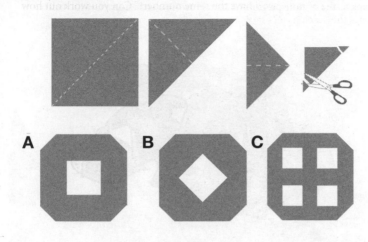

A   B   C

Answer on page 161

LATIN SQUARE: Complete the grid so that every row and column, and every outlined area, contains the letters A, B, C, D, E and F

				F	B
D					A
				D	
A		C			
			E		
	A				E

Answer on page 161

33

RIDDLE: A fish is 45 centimetres long, and its head is as long as its tail. If its head were twice as long as it really is, the head and tail together would be as long as the middle part of the fish. How long is each part of the fish?

Answer on page 161

BITS AND PIECES: Can you match the four
broken windows with the pieces of glass below?

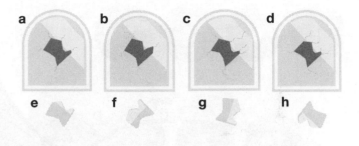

Answer on page 161

MATRIX: Which of the boxed figures completes the set?

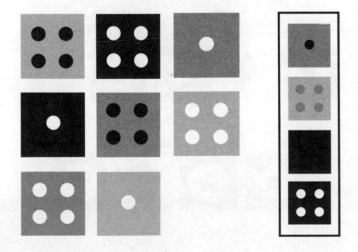

Answer on page 161

NEXT!: Which of the balls, A, B, C or D is the logical next step in this sequence?

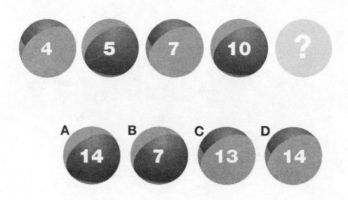

Answer on page 162

NEXT!: Which of the balls, A, B, C or D is the logical next step in this sequence?

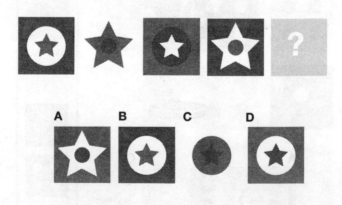

Answer on page 162

BLOCK PARTY: Assuming all blocks that are not visible from this angle are present, how many blocks have been removed from this 6 × 6 × 6 cube?

Answer on page 162

PICTURE PARTS: Which box has exactly the right bits to make the pic?

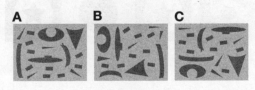

A   **B**   **C**

Answer on page 162

POTS OF DOTS: How many dots should there be in
the hole in this pattern?

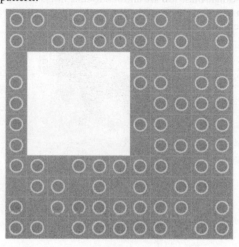

Answer on page 162

SUM TOTAL: Replace the question marks with
mathematical symbols (+, −, × or ÷) to make a working sum.

$$9 ? 2 ? 3 ? 9 = 6$$

Answer on page 162

RIDDLE: You are in a room, blindfolded, with a bowl containing 50, 20, 10 and 5 dollar bills. You are allowed to take notes out of the bowl one at a time until you have four notes of the same value. What's the largest amount of cash you could end up with?

Answer on page 162

BLOCK PARTY: Assuming all blocks that are not visible from this angle are present, how many blocks have been removed from this 5 × 5 × 5 cube?

Answer on page 162

BOXES:
In the game of boxes, each player takes it in turns to join two adjacent dots with a line. If a player's line completes a box, the player wins the box and has another go. It's your turn in the game below. Can you give your opponent just one box?

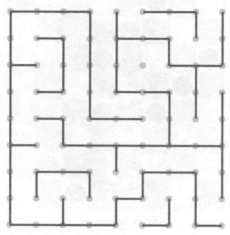

Answer on page 162

DOUBLE DRAT:
All these letters appear twice in the box except one. Can you spot the singleton?

Answer on page 163

40

CHECKERS: Make a move for white so that eight black pieces are left, none of which are in the same column or row.

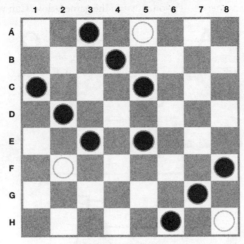

Answer on page 163

BOXES: In the game of boxes, each player takes it in turns to join two adjacent dots with a line. If a player's line completes a box, the player wins the box and has another go. It's your turn in the game below. Can you give your opponent just one box?

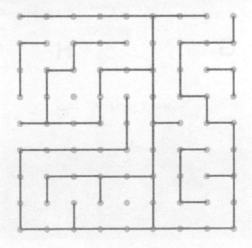

Answer on page 163

41

DRESSING SNOWMAN: Arrange this set
of snowman pics in the correct order from bare ball of snow to fully fledged.

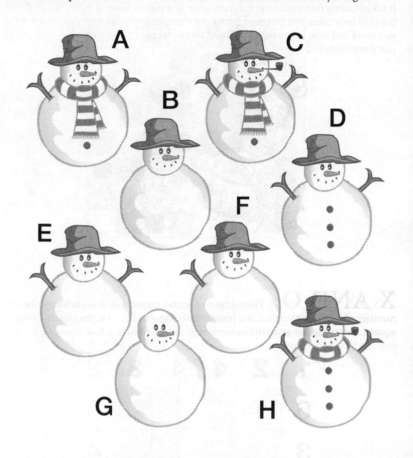

Answer on page 163

RIDDLE:

Celebrity chef Gordon Ramsfoot discovered one Sunday morning that his toaster had broken and he had three hungry kids on his hands. It takes exactly one minute to toast one side of a piece of bread using the grill, but the grill only takes two pieces of bread at a time. In a terrible hurry as always, can you work out how he managed to make three pieces of toast, using the grill, in just three minutes?

Answer on page 163

X AND O:

The numbers around the edge of the grid describe the number of X's in the vertical, horizontal and diagonal lines connecting with that square. Complete the grid so that there is an X or O in every square.

1	2	4	4	3	2
6					4
3					4
2		X			3
2			X		1
2	3	2	2	5	1

Answer on page 163

43

IN THE AREA: Can you work out the approximate area this letter Q is taking up?

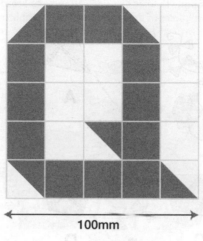

100mm

Answer on page 163

THINK OF A NUMBER: Officers Kaplutski and Wojowitz like a doughnut while they work. On a week long stakeout, Kaplutski ate 12 jam doughnuts and Wojowitz ate 28. What percentage of all the doughnuts eaten did Wojowitz account for?

Answer on page 163

MIRROR IMAGE: Only one of these pictures is an exact mirror image of the first one? Can you spot it?

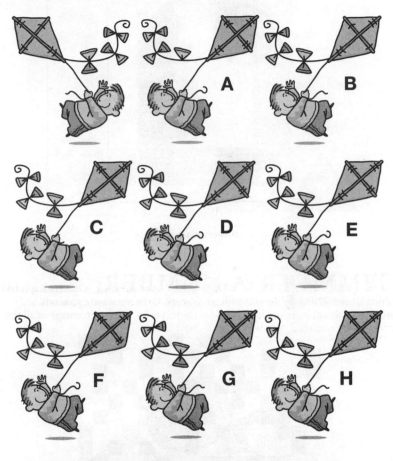

Answer on page 164

MATRIX: Which of the boxed figures completes the set?

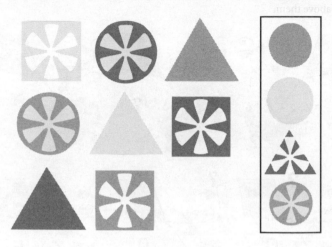

Answer on page 164

SYMMETRY: This picture, when finished, is symmetrical along a vertical line up the middle. Can you colour in the missing squares and work out what the picture is of?

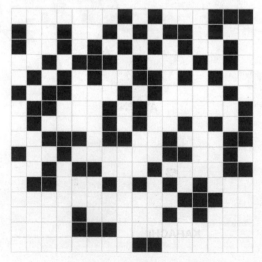

Answer on page 164

NUMBER MOUNTAIN: Replace the
question marks with numbers so that each pair of blocks adds up to the block
directly above them.

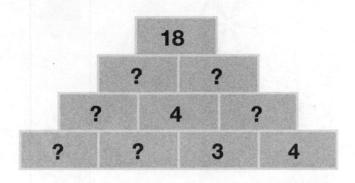

Answer on page 164

ODD CLOCKS: Paris is 2 hours behind Athens, which is
2 hours behind Karachi. It is 1.50 am on Sunday in Athens – what time is it in the
other two cities?

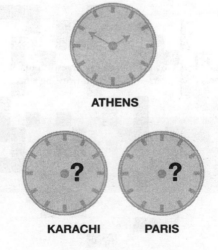

ATHENS

KARACHI   **PARIS**

Answer on page 164

PICTURE PARTS: Which box contains exactly the right bits to make the pic?

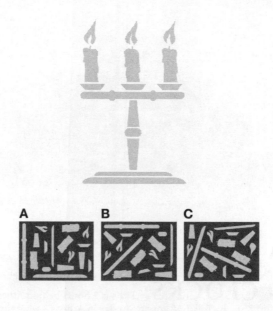

A   B   C

Answer on page 164

SUM TOTAL: Replace the question marks with mathematical symbols (+, –, × or ÷) to make a working sum.

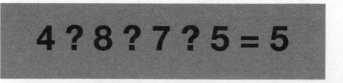

$$4 ? 8 ? 7 ? 5 = 5$$

Answer on page 164

PICTURE PARTS: Which box contains exactly the right bits to make the pic?

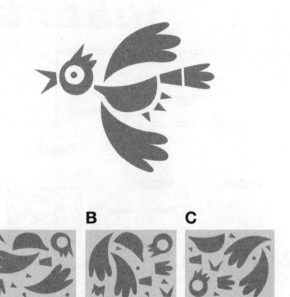

A **B** **C**

49

SCALES:
The arms of these scales are divided into sections – a weight two sections away from the middle will be twice as heavy as a weight one section away. Can you arrange the supplied weights in such a way as to balance the whole scale?

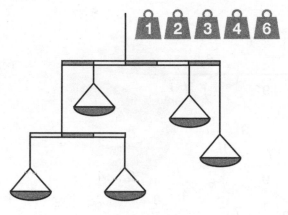

Answer on page 165

SUM PEOPLE:
Work out what number is represented by which person and replace the question mark.

Answer on page 165

PAINT BY NUMBERS: Colour in the odd

numbers to reveal... What?

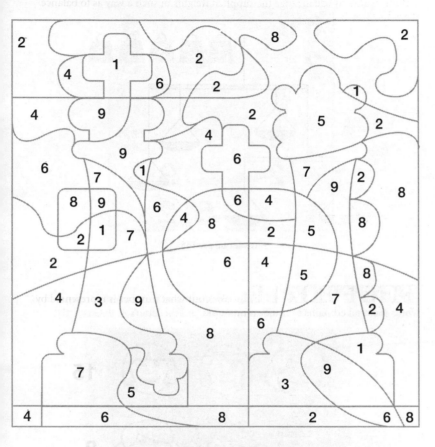

Answer on page 165

SUDOKU SIXPACK: Complete the grid so that
every row, column and long diagonal contains the numbers 1, 2, 3, 4, 5 and 6.

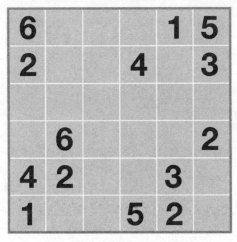

Answer on page 165

SHUFFLE: Fill in the shuffle box so that each row, column and
long diagonal contains four different shapes and the letters A, B, C and D.

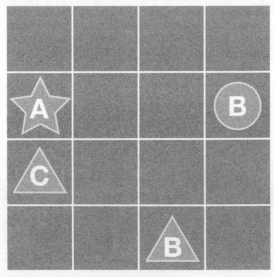

Answer on page 165

SHUFFLE: Fill in the grid so that each row, column and long diagonal contains four different shapes and the letters A, B, C and D.

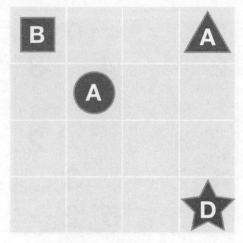

Answer on page 165

SHAPE STACKER: Can you work out the logic behind the numbers in these shapes, and suggest a number to replace the question mark?

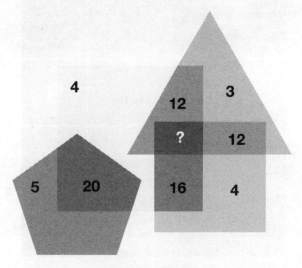

Answer on page 166

53

SHAPE SHIFTING: Fill in the empty squares so
that each row, column and long diagonal contains five different symbols.

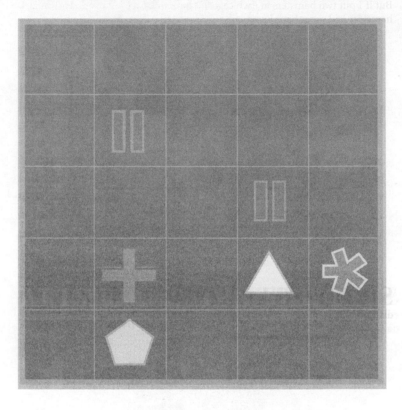

Answer on page 166

RIDDLE: In my shed at home I have some hamsters and some hamster cages. If I put one hamster in each cage I'd have one hamster too many. But if I put two hamsters in each cage, I'd have one cage left over... How many hamsters and cages have I got?

Answer on page 166

SIGNPOST: Can you crack the logical secret behind the distances to these great cities, and work out how far it is to Karachi?

NEW YORK 11

OSLO 2

KARACHI ?

PARIS 5

GDANSK 13

Answer on page 166

MEDIUM
PUZZLES

BOXES:

Playing the game of boxes, each player takes it in turns to join two adjacent dots with a line. If a player's line completes a box, the player wins the box and has another go. It's your turn in the game below. To avoid giving your opponent a lot of boxes, what's your best move?

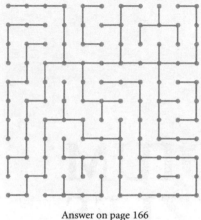

Answer on page 166

CUT AND FOLD:

Which of the patterns below is created by this fold and cut?

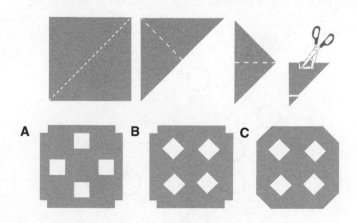

A B C

Answer on page 166

MAGIC SQUARES: Complete the square using nine consecutive numbers, so that all rows, columns and large diagonals add up to the same total.

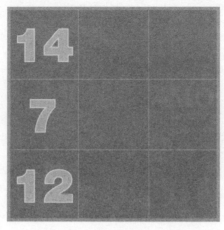

Answer on page 167

MASYU: Draw a single unbroken line around the grid that passes through all the circles. The line must enter and leave each box in the centre of one of its four sides. **Black Circle:** Turn left or right in the box, and the line must pass straight through the next and previous boxes. **White Circle:** Travel straight through the box, and the line must turn in the next and/or previous box.

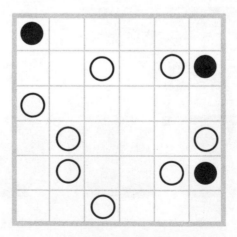

Answer on page 167

RIDDLE: Kitty has fallen down a well 12 metres (that's about 35 feet in old money) deep. He can jump 3 metres up. But slides back 2 metres every time he lands. How many jumps get kitty out of the well?

Answer on page 167

THINK OF A NUMBER: At the Sea View Guest house in Bournemouth, England over the course of one week they served 351 glasses of fruit juice with breakfast. 203 of them were orange, 31 were grapefruit, 39 were mango and 78 were apple. Can you work out what proportion of guests had citrus as opposed to non-citrus juices?

Answer on page 167

SUM PEOPLE: Work out what number is represented by which person and fill in the question mark.

Answer on page 167

TENTS AND TREES: Every tree has one tent found horizontally or vertically adjacent to it. No tent can be in an adjacent square to another tent (even diagonally!). The numbers by each row and column tell you how many tents there are. Can you locate all the tents?

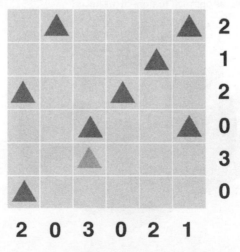

Answer on page 167

SIGNPOST: Can you crack the logical secret behind the distances to these great cities, and work out how far it is to Washington?

Answer on page 167

BLOCK PARTY: Assuming all blocks that are not visible from this angle are present, how many blocks have been removed from this 6 x 6 x 6 cube?

Answer on page 167

61

WHERE'S THE PAIR: Only two of the shapes below are exactly the same – can you find the matching pair?

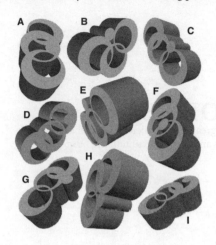

Answer on page 168

DOUBLE DRAT: All these shapes appear twice in the box except one. Can you spot the singleton?

Answer on page 168

"Growing older is not upsetting; being perceived as old is."

KENNY ROGERS

MORE OR LESS: The arrows indicate whether a
number in a box is greater or smaller than an adjacent number. Complete the
grid so that all rows and columns contain the numbers 1 to 5.

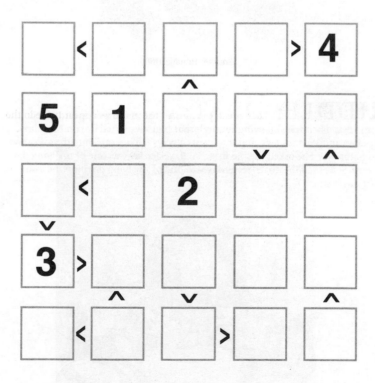

Answer on page 168

PERCENTAGE POINT: What percentage of
this grid is darker and what percentage is lighter?

Answer on page 168

RIDDLE: Lucy met a pig and a goat in the woods and asked
them what day it was, knowing full well that pigs always tell lies on Mondays,
Tuesdays and Wednesdays, and that goats always tell lies on Thursdays, Fridays
and Saturdays. She asked the pig first. 'Well, yesterday was one of my lying days,'
he said. She asked the goat. 'Yesterday was one of my lying days too,' he said... So
what day is it?

Answer on page 168

BOX IT:

The value of each shape is the number of sides each shape has, multiplied by the number within it. Thus a square containing the number 4 has a value of 16. Find a block two squares wide and two squares high with a total value of exactly 50.

Answer on page 168

BOXES:

Playing the game of boxes, each player takes it in turns to join two adjacent dots with a line. If a player's line completes a box, the player wins the box and has another go. It's your turn in the game below. To avoid giving your opponent a lot of boxes, what's your best move?

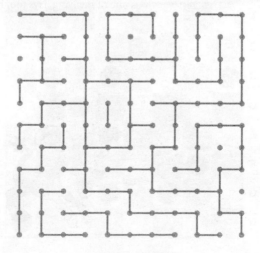

Answer on page 168

TENTS AND TREES: Every tree has one tent
found horizontally or vertically adjacent to it. No tent can be in an adjacent
square to another tent (even diagonally). The numbers by each row and column
tell you how many tents there are. Can you locate all the tents?

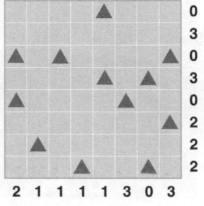

Answer on page 169

CHECKERS: Make a move for white so that eight black pieces
are left, none of which are in the same column or row.

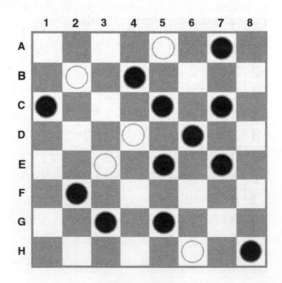

Answer on page 169

DICE PUZZLE: What's the missing number?

15   12   16   ?

Answer on page 169

FIGURE IT OUT: The sequence 23224 can be found
once in the grid, reading up, down, backwards, forwards or diagonally. Can you
pick it out?

4	2	2	3	4	4	4	4	3	4	4	4
4	4	3	4	2	2	2	2	2	2	2	2
2	3	2	2	3	3	3	2	4	3	3	3
3	2	3	2	2	3	2	2	2	2	2	2
3	4	3	2	2	2	4	3	2	2	4	2
3	3	2	2	3	3	4	2	2	3	2	2
4	3	2	2	2	2	2	3	2	2	3	3
2	4	3	3	4	3	2	2	3	4	3	4
3	4	4	4	2	2	2	3	2	2	2	2
4	2	2	2	2	3	3	2	4	3	3	3
2	4	3	2	4	4	4	4	2	2	2	2
3	2	3	2	2	3	4	3	3	2	3	4

Answer on page 169

GAME OF THREE HALVES:

Which three shapes below will piece together to create the top shape?

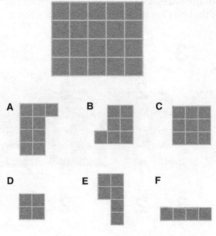

Answer on page 169

LATIN SQUARE Complete the grid so that every row and column, and every outlined area, contains the letters A, B, C, D, E and F.

E					
	B			D	
C			A		
					C
F		B		E	

Answer on page 169

LOOPLINK:
Connect adjacent dots with either horizontal or vertical lines to create a continuous unbroken loop which never crosses over itself. Some, but not all of the boxes are numbered. The numbers in these boxes tell you how many sides of that box are used by your unbroken line.

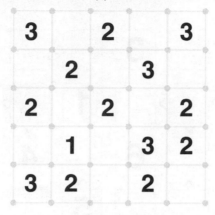

Answer on page 169

MASYU:
Draw a single unbroken line around the grid that passes through all the circles. The line must enter and leave each box in the centre of one of its four sides. **Black Circle:** Turn left or right in the box, and the line must pass straight through the next and previous boxes. **White Circle:** Travel straight through the box, and the line must turn in the next and/or previous box.

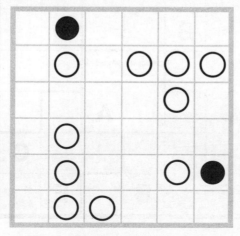

Answer on page 169

MORE OR LESS:

The arrows indicate whether a number in a box is greater or smaller than an adjacent number. Complete the grid so that all rows and columns contain the numbers 1 to 6.

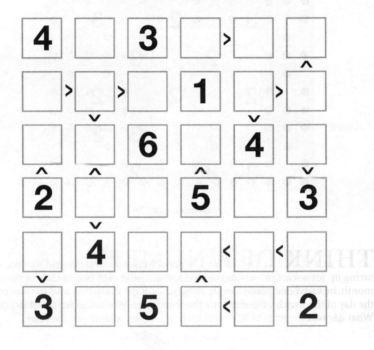

Answer on page 170

POTS OF DOTS: How many dots should there be in
the hole in this pattern?

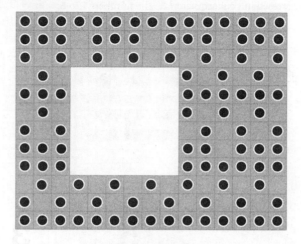

Answer on page 170

THINK OF A NUMBER: Little Joe was
saving up for a scarf to wear to the big football match. On the first day of the
month, he saved one penny, on the second, 2, on the third, 3 and so on until on
the day of the match he had exactly the three pounds required to buy the scarf.
What day was the game?

Answer on page 170

SAFECRACKER:
To open the safe, all the buttons must be pressed in the correct order before the "open" button is pressed. What is the first button pressed in your sequence?

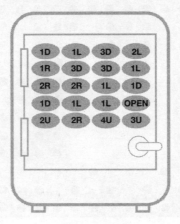

Answer on page 170

SCALES:
The arms of these scales are divided into sections – a weight two sections away from the middle will be twice as heavy as a weight one section away. Can you arrange the supplied weights in such a way as to balance the whole scale?

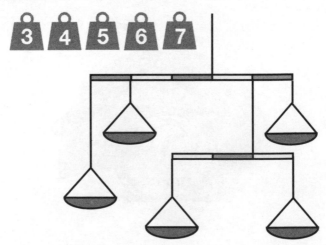

Answer on page 170

SHAPE SHIFTING: Fill in the empty squares so that each row, column and long diagonal contains five different numbered balls.

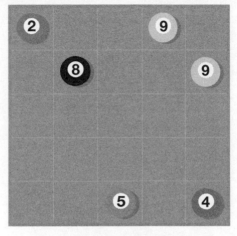

Answer on page 170

SIGNPOST: Can you crack the logical secret behind the distances to these great cities, and work out how far it is to Vancouver?

Answer on page 170

SUDOKU SIXPACK: Complete the grid so that
every row, column and long diagonal contains the numbers 1, 2, 3, 4, 5 and 6.

	6		3		
6					2
	1		2		
5		6	1	4	
	5		4		
		4		2	

Answer on page 171

SUM PEOPLE: Work out what number is represented by
which person and fill in the question mark.

Answer on page 171

74

SUDOKU: Complete the grid so that all rows and columns, and each outlined block of nine squares, contain the numbers 1, 2, 3, 4, 5, 6, 7, 8 and 9.

		2		1		4		
	5	1		9		7	3	8
7				6		2		
					1		4	5
3				8		9		1
1		4	7					
				4		8		7
4		6	8		2	1	9	
	3					5		

Answer on page 171

THINK OF A NUMBER: Officers Kaplutski
and Wojowitz were counting up how many jaywalkers they had arrested in a
week. Kaplutski was happy to discover he was ahead 14 to 11. Can you express the
two cop's success rate as a percentage?

Answer on page 171

VENN DIAGRAMS: Can you work out which areas
of this diagram represent Australian teetotal surfers who don't play rugby, and
non-Australian beer drinking rugby players that don't surf?

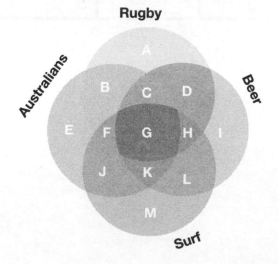

Answer on page 171

"Like beauty, age is in the eye of the beholder."

ANON

BITS AND PIECES: These ten pieces can be asembled to spell the name of a movie star... Who?

Answer on page 171

FINDING NEMO:
The word NEMO can be found once in the grid, reading up, down, backwards, forwards or diagonally. Can you pick it out?

Answer on page 171

MAGIC SQUARES:
Complete the square using nine consecutive numbers, so that all rows, columns and large diagonals add up to the same total.

Answer on page 171

MATRIX: Which of the boxed figures completes the set?

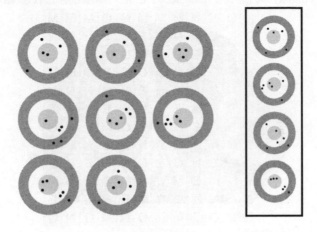

Answer on page 172

ODD CLOCKS: Auckland is 16 hours ahead of Sao Paulo, which is 1 hour ahead of Miami. It is 2.15 pm on Saturday in Sao Paulo – what time is it in the other two cities?

SAO PAULO

MIAMI   **AUCKLAND**

Answer on page 172

RIDDLE:
Jessica promised Julia that she would tell her a huge piece of gossip, but it would have to wait until the day before four days from the day after tomorrow. Today is Wednesday the 3rd – when does Julia get to know?

Answer on page 172

SAFECRACKER:
To open the safe, all the buttons must be pressed in the correct order before the "open" button is pressed. What is the first button pressed in your sequence?

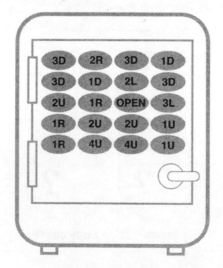

3D	2R	3D	1D
3D	1D	2L	3D
2U	1R	OPEN	3L
1R	2U	2U	1U
1R	4U	4U	1U

Answer on page 172

LOGIC SEQUENCE: The balls below have been

rearranged. Can you work out the new sequence of the balls from the clues given below?

The 4 ball isn't touching the 5 or the 2.
The 8 ball is touching four others.
The 4 ball is immediately to the right of the 6.
The 10 ball is resting on two balls totalling 13.

Answer on page 172

BOXES: Playing the game of boxes, each player takes it in turns to

join two adjacent dots with a line. If a player's line completes a box, the player wins the box and has another go. It's your turn in the game below. To avoid giving your opponent a lot of boxes, what's your best move?

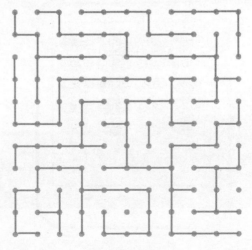

Answer on page 172

X AND O:

The numbers around the edge of the grid describe the number of X's in the vertical, horizontal and diagonal lines connecting with that square. Complete the grid so that there is an X or O in every square.

2	4	5	4	2	7	1
5	X			X		4
4						3
3						6
2			O			4
5	O			X		5
1	2	4	3	4	6	2

Answer on page 173

WRINKLY QUOTE

"Age is a matter of feeling, not of years."

GEORGE WILLIAM CURTIS

PERCENTAGE POINT: What percentage of
this shape is darker and what percentage is lighter?

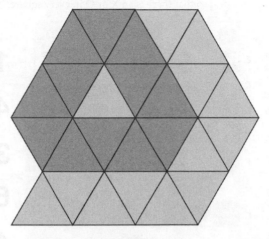

Answer on page 173

POTS OF DOTS: How many dots should there be in
the hole in this pattern?

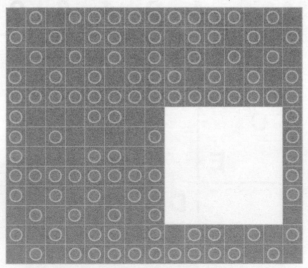

Answer on page 173

CHECKERS: Make a move for white so that eight black pieces are left, none of which are in the same column or row.

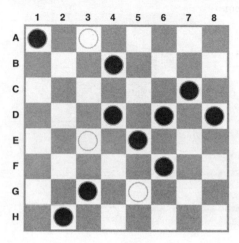

Answer on page 173

LATIN SQUARE: Complete the grid so that every row and column, and every outlined area, contains the letters A, B, C, D, E and F.

F					D
			A		E
C					
	E				
		D			
E		B			C

Answer on page 173

NUMBER MOUNTAIN: Replace the
question marks with numbers so that each pair of blocks adds up to the block
directly above them.

Answer on page 173

PICTURE PARTS: Which box has exactly the right
bits to make the pic?

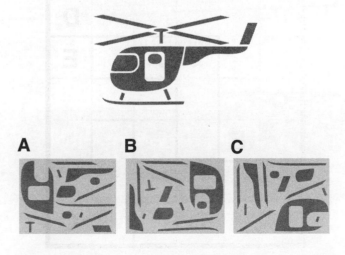

Answer on page 173

85

THINK OF A NUMBER: Belinda, Benny,

Bobby, Brian and Bill entered a competition to guess how many sweets there were in a jar. Belinda said 300, Ben said 280, Bobby said 290, Brian said 250 and Bill said 260. Two guesses were just ten sweets away from the number. One guess was 40 away and another was wrong by 30. But who won?

Answer on page 174

Answer on page 174

SUM PEOPLE: Work out what number is represented by which person and fill in the question mark.

				21
				34
				14
				16
21	**?**	**27**	**15**	

Answer on page 174

THINK OF A NUMBER: Old Mother

Jones loves her gummy sweets. They come in three colours: orange, red and yellow. There were exactly twice as many red sweets as yellow ones in the packet. After eating seven orange ones, she had one less orange than yellow left, and the number of orange sweets remaining represented 20 percent of the sweets she started with. How many did she start with?

Answer on page 174

SHUFFLE: Fill up the shuffle box so that each row, column and long diagonal contains a Jack, Queen, King and Ace of each suit.

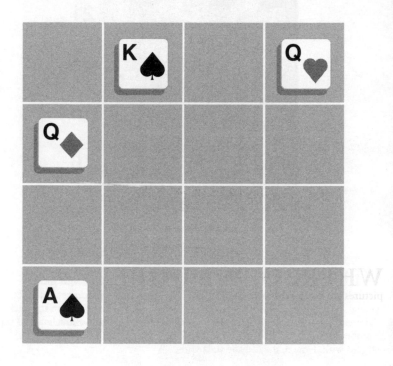

Answer on page 174

DOUBLE DRAT: All these shapes appear twice in the box except one. Can you spot the singleton?

Answer on page 174

WHERE'S THE PAIR?: Only two of these pictures are exactly the same. Can you spot the matching pair?

Answer on page 174

THE RED CORNER: Use the numbers in the corners to make the central number the same way in all three cases. What number should replace the question mark?

Answer on page 175

HUB SIGNS: What numbers should appear in the hubs of these number wheels?

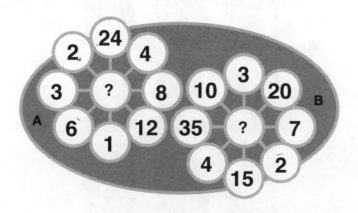

Answer on page 175

BOX IT:
The value of each shape is the number of sides each shape has, multiplied by the number within it. Thus a square containing the number 4 has a value of 16. Find a block two squares wide and two squares high with a total value of exactly 100.

Answer on page 175

REVOLUTIONS:
Cog A has 10 teeth, cog B has 8 and cog C has 14. How many revolutions must cog A turn through to bring all three cogs back to these exact positions?

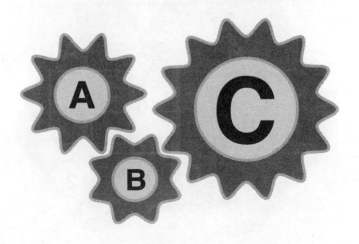

Answer on page 175

THINK OF A NUMBER:
Ada the antique dealer was pondering her profits one day, and thinking how she could improve them. She looked at the Victorian clock she was selling for a 5% profit, and worked out that had she bought it for 10% less and sold it at the same price she would have made a £15 profit. How much did she buy it for?

Answer on page 175

WHERE'S THE PAIR?:
Only two of the shapes below are exactly the same. Can you find the matching pair?

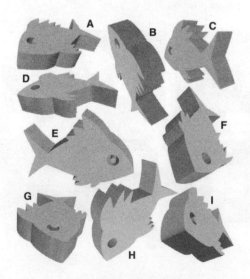

Answer on page 175

CATS AND COGS: Turn the handle in the indicated direction... Does the cat go up or down?

Answer on page 175

CUT AND FOLD: Which of the patterns below is created by this fold and cut?

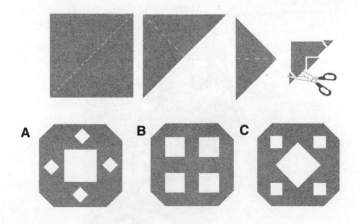

A   B   C

Answer on page 175

MORE OR LESS:
The arrows indicate whether a number in a box is greater or smaller than an adjacent number. Complete the grid so that all rows and columns contain the numbers 1 to 6.

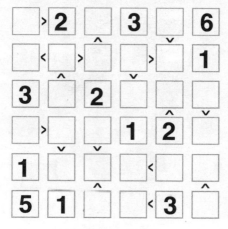

Answer on page 175

RIDDLE:
Mr and Mrs Toggle were driving from Aystown to Beestown on vacation when Mr T accidentally ran down a signpost at a road junction. The post was fine, completely unharmed. But how do they know which way Beestown is now?

Answer on page 175

SHAPE SHIFTING: Fill in the empty squares so that each row, column and long diagonal contains six different symbols.

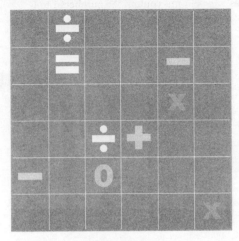

Answer on page 176

BLOCK PARTY: Assuming all blocks that are not visible from this angle are present, how many blocks have been removed from this 5 x 5 x 5 cube?

Answer on page 176

DOUBLE MAZE: Make your way from A to B without passing through any lighter squares – then do it again without passing through any darker squares!

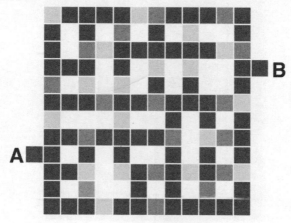

Answer on page 176

RADAR: The numbers in some cells in the grid indicate the exact number of black cells that should border it. Shade these black, until all the numbers are surrounded by the correct number of black cells.

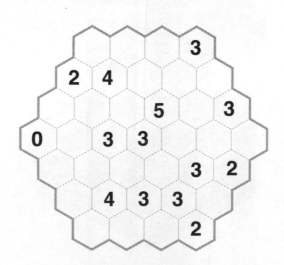

Answer on page 176

SHUFFLE: Fill up the shuffle box so that each row, column and long diagonal contains a Jack, Queen, King and Ace of each suit.

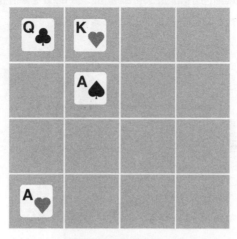

Answer on page 176

SILHOUETTE: Which of the fish matches our silhouette?

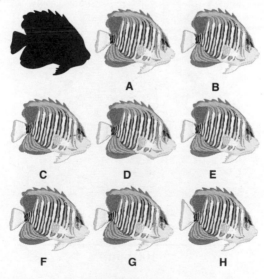

Answer on page 176

97

SYMBOL SUMS: These symbols represent the numbers
1 to 4. If the lightly shaded parrot represents the number 2, can you work out
what the other shaded parrots are representing and make a working sum?

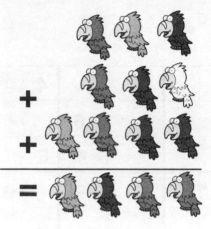

Answer on page 176

IN THE AREA: Can you work out the approximate area
that this camel is occupying?

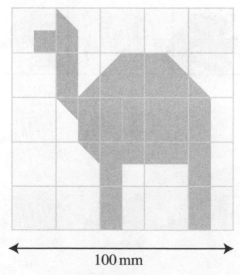

100 mm

Answer on page 176

SUDOKU:
Complet the grid so that all rows and columns, and each outlined block of nine squares, contain the numbers 1, 2, 3, 4, 5, 6, 7, 8 and 9.

5	1			2		4	9	8
	3		1		6		7	5
	8				4	6		
	7	3			9		8	
1				7		9		2
	2		3		5	1		
	5		8	6			4	
	9	2					5	6
8		4		9	7	3		

Answer on page 177

SUDOKU SIXPACK: Complete the grid so that

every row, column and long diagonal contains the numbers 1, 2, 3, 4, 5 and 6.

	5		6	4	3
4					5
6					
		6	1	5	
1	2	4		3	
		2			

Answer on page 177

FLOOR FILLERS: Below is a plan of the entrance

pathway to a theatre, complete with spaces either side for plant pots. Below it are some oddly shaped pieces of red carpet... Can you fill the floor with them?

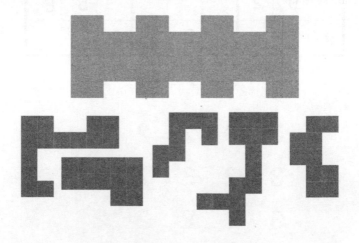

Answer on page 177

TENTS AND TREES:
Every tree has one tent found horizontally or vertically adjacent to it. No tent can be in an adjacent square to another tent (even diagonally!). The numbers by each row and column tell you how many tents there are. Can you locate all the tents?

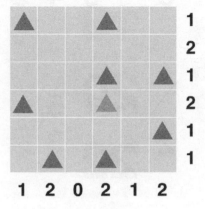

Answer on page 177

LOOPLINK:
Connect adjacent dots with either horizontal or vertical lines to create a continuous unbroken loop which never crosses over itself. The numbers in these boxes tell you how many sides of that box are used by your unbroken line.

3	2	2	2	3
3	1	1	2	2
3	0	2	2	2
3	2	3	2	3
3	1	2	2	2

Answer on page 177

MAGIC SQUARES: Complete the square using nine consecutive numbers, so that all rows, columns and large diagonals add up to the same total.

Answer on page 177

SHAPE STACKER: Can you work out the logic behind the numbers in these shapes, and suggest what number the question mark represents?

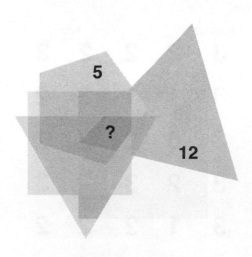

Answer on page 177

ODD CLOCKS: Rio is six hours behind Athens, which is two hours behind Karachi. It is 1.25 am on Thursday in Athens – what time is it in the other two cities?

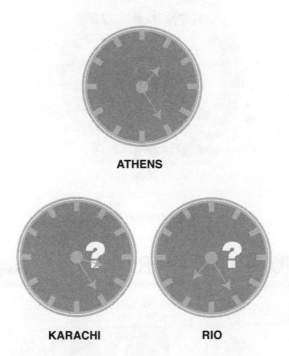

ATHENS

KARACHI

RIO

Answer on page 178

SIGNPOST: Can you crack the logical secret behind the distances to these great cities, and work out how far it is to Hong Kong?

NEW YORK 28

GLASGOW 14

HONG KONG ?

BARCELONA 8

COLOMBO 9

Answer on page 178

MIRROR IMAGE: Only one of these pictures is an exact mirror image of the first one? Can you spot it?

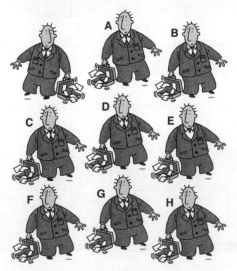

Answer on page 178

NUMBER SWEEP: The numbers in some squares

in the grid indicate the exact number of black squares that should surround it. Shade these squares until all the numbers are surrounded by the correct number of black squares, and a number will be revealed!

0	2		5		5		5		5		2
	4			8		8		8		5	
2		7	8		6		5		5		2
	5		8			6		6		3	
4		8		7	6		5		4		1
	7		7		5			7		5	
3		5		4		3	5		8		4
	6		4		0		3			8	
3		5		4		3		6	8		5
	7		7		5		6		8		
3		6		8		8		7		4	3
	2		4		5		5		4		1

Answer on page 178

SCALES: The arms of these scales are divided into sections – a

weight two sections away from the middle will be twice as heavy as a weight one section away. Can you arrange the supplied weights in such a way as to balance the whole scale?

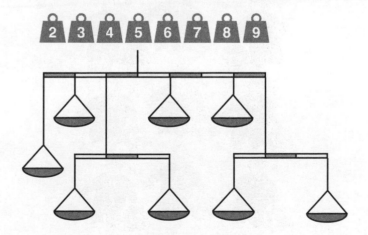

Answer on page 178

HARD
PUZZLES

MINESWEEPER: The numbers in some squares in the grid indicate the exact number of black squares that should surround it. Shade these squares until all the numbers are surrounded by the correct number of black squares.

0			1	2			2
1		2	1				2
		2		2	2	2	
2		2					0
	1	1	2		2	1	
2		1		2		2	1
	3			3	5		3
2		2	2				

Answer on page 178

WHERE'S THE PAIR?: Only two of the shapes below are exactly the same. Can you find the matching pair?

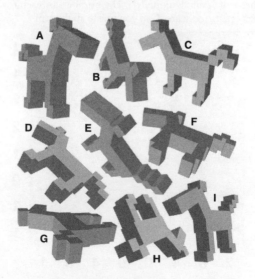

Answer on page 178

107

MASYU: Draw a single continuous line around the grid that passes through all the circles. The line must enter and leave each box in the centre of one of its four sides. **Black Circle:** Turn left or right in the box, and the line must pass straight through the next and previous boxes. **White Circle:** Travel straight through the box, and the line must turn in the next and/or previous box.

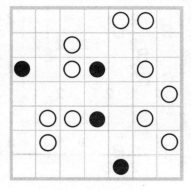

Answer on page 178

TENTS AND TREES: Every tree has one tent found horizontally or vertically adjacent to it. No tent can be in an adjacent square to another tent (even diagonally!). The numbers by each row and column tell you how many tents there are. Can you locate all the tents?

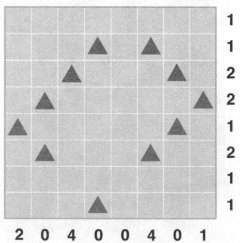

Answer on page 179

CODOKU SIX:
Complete the first grid so that every row and column contains all the letters BCIMU and W. Do the same with grid 2 and the numbers 12345 and 6. To decode the finished grid, add the numbers in the shaded squares to the letters in the matching squares in the first grid (ie: A + 3 = D, Y + 4 = C) to get six new letters which can be arranged to spell the name of a city.

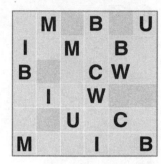

Answer on page 179

CUBE VOLUME:
These little cubes originally made a big 5 x 5 x 5 cube measuring 20 cm × 20 cm × 20 cm. Now some of the little cubes have been removed, can you work out what volume the remaining cubes have now? Assume all invisible cubes are present.

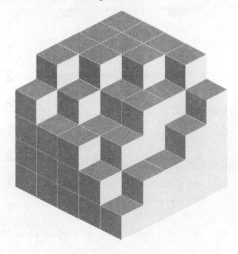

Answer on page 179

WHERE'S THE PAIR?: Only two of these
pictures are exactly the same. Can you spot the matching pair?

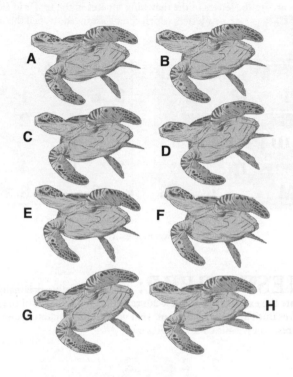

Answer on page 179

PERCENTAGE POINT: Can you determine
what percentage of this honeycomb is occupied by bees, and what percentage of the bees are awake?

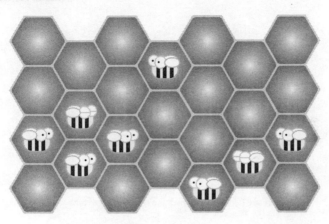

Answer on page 179

MINESWEEPER: The numbers in some squares in the
grid indicate the exact number of black squares that should surround it. Shade these squares until all the numbers are surrounded by the correct number of black squares.

	2	2		2	3		3
2			3				
	3	3		2	3		3
3			3	3		2	2
	3	4			1	2	
1				3			
2	4	4	3		2		
			1	1		2	1

Answer on page 179

LOGIC SEQUENCE: The balls below have been

rearranged. Can you work out the new sequence of the balls from the clues given below?

The square is immediately to the right of the X.

The circle is between the X and the triangle.

There are two balls between the circle and the star.

Answer on page 179

A PIECE OF PIE: Can you crack the pie code and work

out what number belongs where the question mark is?

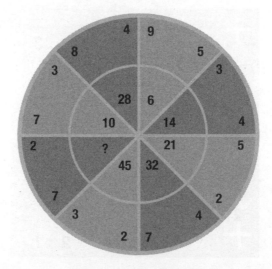

Answer on page 179

FIVE-POINT PROBLEM: Discover the

pattern behind the numbers on these pentagons and fill in the blanks to complete the puzzle.

Answer on page 180

THE GREAT DIVIDE: Divide up the grid

into four equal sized, equally shaped parts, each containing one each of the four different symbols.

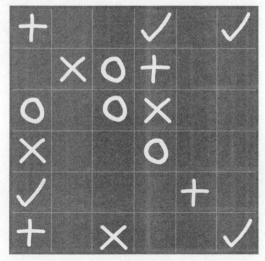

Answer on page 180

KILLER SIX: Complete the grid so that all rows and columns contain the numbers 1, 2, 3, 4, 5 and 6. Areas with a dotted outline contain numbers that add up to the total shown.

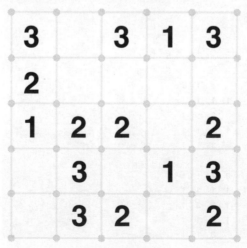

11	16			3	10
	4		4		
13	5			11	
		6	4		11
3			7		
	11			7	

Answer on page 180

LOOPLINK: Connect adjacent dots with either horizontal or vertical lines to create a continuous unbroken loop which never crosses over itself. Some, but not all of the boxes are numbered. The numbers in these boxes tell you how many sides of that box are used by your unbroken line.

3		3	1	3
2				
1	2	2		2
	3		1	3
	3	2		2

Answer on page 180

MASYU:
Draw a single continuous line around the grid that passes through all the circles. The line must enter and leave each box in the centre of one of its four sides. **Black Circle:** Turn left or right in the box, and the line must pass straight through the next and previous boxes. **White Circle:** Travel straight through the box, and the line must turn in the next and/or previous box.

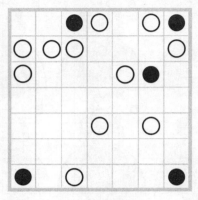

Answer on page 180

MINI NONOGRAM:
The numbers by each row and column describe black squares and groups of black squares that are adjoining. Colour in all the black squares and a six number combination will be revealed.

				1									
				1									
				1									
			5	1	5			5				1	
			5	1	5		3	1	5		1	5	5
	3	1	3										
1	1	1	1										
	3	1	1										
1	1	1	1										
	3	1	1										
3	1	1	1										
1	1	1	1	1									
	1	1	3	1									
	1	1	1	1									
		3	1	1									

Answer on page 180

MIRROR IMAGE: Only one of these pictures is an exact mirror image of the first one? Can you spot it?

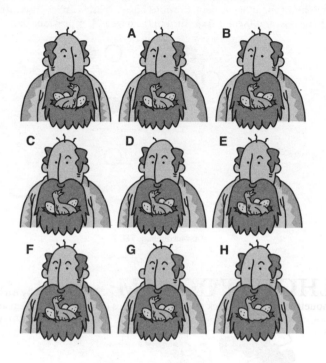

Answer on page 180

SHAPE STACKER: Can you work out the logic behind the numbers in these shapes, and the total of A x B x C?

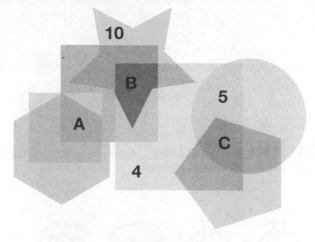

Answer on page 181

SILHOUETTE: Which of the coloured-in pics matches our silhouette?

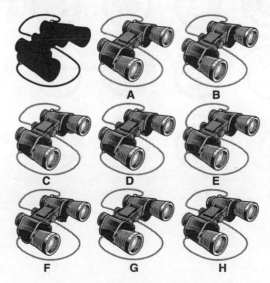

Answer on page 181

"My grandfather always said that living is like licking honey off a thorn."

LOUIS ADAMIC

SUM PEOPLE: Work out what number is represented by which person and replace the question mark.

Answer on page 181

SUM PEOPLE: Work out what number is represented by which person and replace the question mark.

32

?

32

12

32 12 26 61

Answer on page 181

WHERE'S THE PAIR?: Only two of the shapes below are exactly the same – can you find the matching pair?

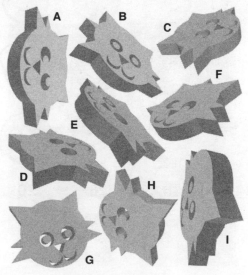

Answer on page 181

CAN YOU CUT IT?: Cut two straight lines

through this shape to create three shapes that are identical.

Answer on page 181

DICE PUZZLE: Which of these dice is not like the other

three?

Answer on page 181

FLOOR FILLERS:
Below is a plan of a bathroom, showing the bath and other fixings, and next to it, some very oddly shaped pieces of marble. Can you arrange them to fill the floor?

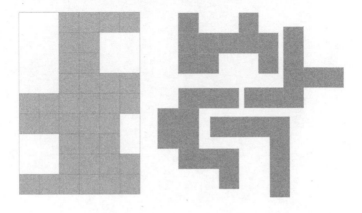

Answer on page 182

HUB SIGNS:
What number should appear in the hub of the second wheel?

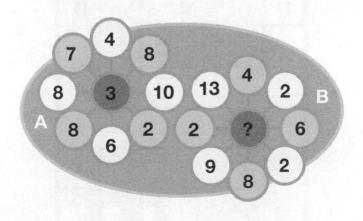

Answer on page 182

JIGSAW: Which four of the pieces below can complete the jigsaw and make a perfect square?

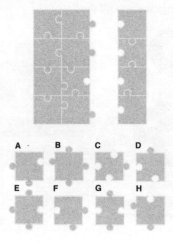

Answer on page 182

LATIN SQUARE: Complete the grid so that every row and column, and every outlined area, contains the letters A, B, C, D, E and F.

B					D
			C		
					E
					F
					A

Answer on page 182

122

LOGIC SEQUENCE: The balls below have been
rearranged. Can you work out the new sequence of the balls from the clues given
below?

The top three balls total 22.
The 5 ball is immediately to the right of the 6,
and isn't in contact with the 4 ball.
The 10 ball touches four others, but not the 6.

Answer on page 182

MINESWEEPER: The numbers in some squares in the
grid indicate the exact number of black squares that should surround it. Shade
these squares until all the numbers are surrounded by the correct number of
black squares.

			2		0	2	
3	4	4					
1			2		3	4	
	1		1	3			2
1	2		3	4		3	
2					3	2	1
	4	5	5		3		
2		2			2	1	1

Answer on page 182

"Becoming a grandmother is great fun because you can use the kid to get back at your daughter."

ROSEANNE BARR

BATTLESHIPS:
The numbers on the side and bottom of the grid indicate occupied squares or groups of consecutive occupied squares in each row or column. Can finish the grid so that it contains three Cruisers, three Launches and three Buoys and the numbers tally?

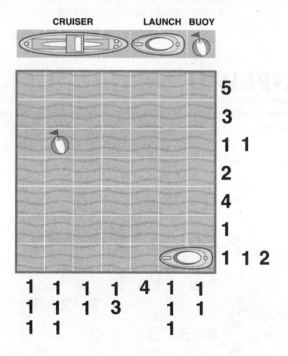

Answer on page 183

TENTS AND TREES: Every tree has one tent

found horizontally or vertically adjacent to it. No tent can be in an adjacent square to another tent (even diagonally!). The numbers by each row and column tell you how many tents there are. Can you locate all the tents?

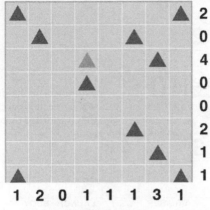

Answer on page 183

LOOPLINK: Connect adjacent dots with either horizontal or

vertical lines to create a continuous unbroken loop which never crosses over itself. Some, but not all of the boxes are numbered. The numbers in these boxes tell you how many sides of that box are used by your unbroken line.

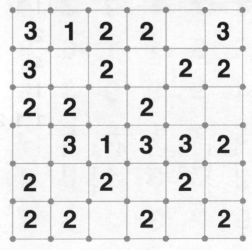

Answer on page 183

125

MORE OR LESS:
The arrows indicate whether a number in a box is greater or smaller than an adjacent number. Complete the grid so that all rows and columns contain the numbers 1 to 6.

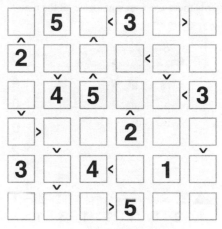

Answer on page 183

NUMBER CHUNKS:
Divide up the grid into four equal size, equally shaped parts, each containing numbers that add up to 40.

8	2	1	2	2	4
6	3	1	1	6	3
4	9	9	9	3	5
5	7	1	5	5	5
2	7	3	1	6	4
9	7	3	2	3	7

Answer on page 183

SAFECRACKER:
To open the safe, all the buttons must be pressed in the correct order before the "open" button is pressed. What is the first button pressed in your sequence?

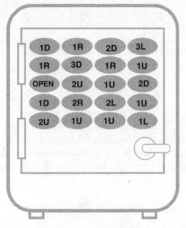

Answer on page 183

SUDOKU:
Complete the grid so that all rows and columns, and each outlined block of nine squares, contain the numbers 1, 2, 3, 4, 5, 6, 7, 8 and 9.

	2		1		8	3		
		7		2				5
4			7			1		
		1	4					8
	9					5		6
2			6	7				
7		6	8					3
8				9			2	
			3				6	4

Answer on page 183

127

"You know an odd feeling? Sitting on the toilet eating a chocolate candy bar."

GEORGE CARLIN

TENTS AND TREES:
Every tree has one tent found horizontally or vertically adjacent to it. No tent can be in an adjacent square to another tent (even diagonally!). The numbers by each row and column tell you how many tents there are. Can you locate all the tents?

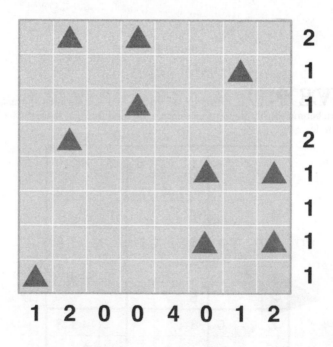

Answer on page 184

CAN YOU CUT IT?: Cut two straight lines
through this shape to create three shapes that are identical.

Answer on page 184

FIVE POINT PROBLEM: Discover the
pattern behind the numbers on these pentagons and fill in the blanks to complete
the puzzle.

Answer on page 184

GRIDLOCK: Which square correctly completes the grid?

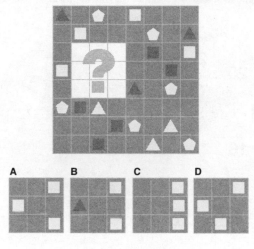

A   B   C   D

Answer on page 184

KILLER SIX: Complete the grid so that all rows and columns
contain the numbers 1, 2, 3, 4, 5 and 6. Areas with a dotted outline contain
numbers that add up to the total shown. Dotted boxes can contan the same
number more than once, however.

9			7		10
16		6			
3		**6**	7	6	
	7			22	
12		11			4
				1	

Answer on page 184

HUB SIGNS: What number should appear in the hub of the second wheel?

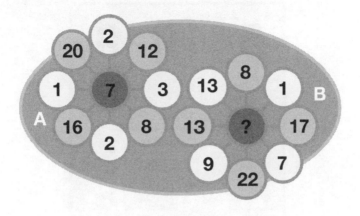

Answer on page 184

LOOPLINK: Connect adjacent dots with either horizontal or vertical lines to create a continuous unbroken loop which never crosses over itself. Some, but not all of the boxes are numbered. The numbers in these boxes tell you how many sides of that box are used by your unbroken line.

1		2		2	2
2	2	3	2		3
	0	3	2	2	2
	3			2	
1		2	2	1	2
3	2	2	2		3

Answer on page 184

MAGIC SQUARES: Complete the square using nine consecutive numbers, so that all rows, columns and large diagonals add up to the same total.

Answer on page 185

THE GREAT DIVIDE: Divide up the grid into four equal size, equally shaped parts, each containing one each of the four different symbols.

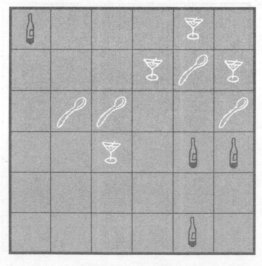

Answer on page 185

SMALL LOGIC:
Little Tom collects insects. Can you discover where he found these three, at what time of day, and what he put them in so he could take them home?

1) The spider was found in the evening, not in a field.
2) The butterfly was found in the forest, though not in the morning, and Tom didn't put it in a jar.
3) The creature found in a field was placed in a bottle.

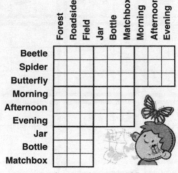

Answer on page 185

SUDOKU:
Complete the grid so that all rows and columns, and each outlined block of nine squares, contain the numbers 1, 2, 3, 4, 5, 6, 7, 8 and 9.

		6		7		5	3	
8			1	3		2		
					2			
9				5			4	
		4			6		8	5
2	8		7	9		6		
	1			6				9
	7					4	2	1
5			4				6	

Answer on page 185

133

SUDOKU: Fill in the numbers 1, 2, 3, 4, 5, 6, 7, 8, and 9 so they appear once only in each row, column and 9 x 9 grid

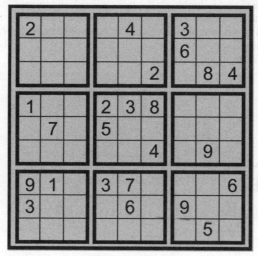

Answer on page 185

THE RED CORNER: Use the corners to make the central number the same way in all three cases. What number should replace the question mark?

Answer on page 185

CODOKU SIX: Complete the first grid so that every row and column contain all the letters ABJKY and Z. Do the same with grid 2 and the numbers 12345 and 6. To decode the finished grid, add the numbers in the shaded squares to the letters in the matching squares in the second (ie: A + 3 = D, Y + 4 = C) to get six new letters which can be arranged to spell the name of a famous composer.

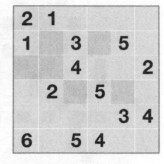

Answer on page 185

NUMBER MOUNTAIN: Replace the question marks with numbers so that each pair of blocks adds up to the block directly above them.

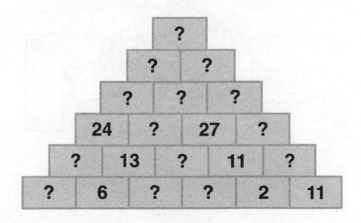

Answer on page 185

SYMMETRY:
This picture, when finished, is symmetrical along a vertical line up the middle. Can you colour in the missing squares and work out what the picture is of?

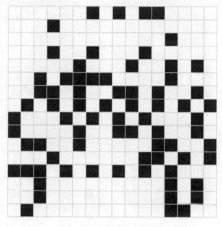

Answer on page 186

CUBE VOLUME:
These little cubes originally made a big 5 x 5 x 5 cube measuring 15 cm x 15 cm x 15 cm. Now some of the little cubes have been removed, can you work out what volume the remaining cubes have? Assume all hidden cubes are present.

Answer on page 186

DICE PUZZLE: Which of these dice is not like the other three?

Answer on page 186

KILLER SIX: Complete the grid so that all rows and columns contain the numbers 1, 2, 3, 4, 5 and 6. Areas with a dotted outline contain numbers that add up to the total shown.

15	4	11		5	
			11		6
	7		**1**	6	
6	**6**	9			11
	9		9	**4**	
				6	

Answer on page 186

MASYU:

Draw a single continuous line around the grid that passes through all the circles. The line must enter and leave each box in the centre of one of its four sides. **Black Circle:** Turn left or right in the box, and the line must pass straight through the next and previous boxes. **White Circle:** Travel straight through the box, and the line must turn in the next and/or previous box.

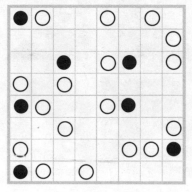

Answer on page 186

MINI NONOGRAM:

The numbers by each row and column describe black squares and groups of black squares that are adjoining. Colour in all the black squares and a six number combination will be revealed.

					1					
		1		3	1	5		5		
		3	5	5	5	1	5	1	1	5
1 1 1 1 1										
1 1 1 1 1										
3 3 1										
1 1 1										
1 1 1										
1 3 3										
1 1 1 1										
1 1 1 1										
1 1 1 1										
1 3 1										

Answer on page 186

NUMBER CHUNKS: Divide up the grid into four equal size, equally shaped parts, each containing numbers that add up to 36.

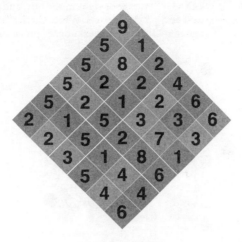

Answer on page 186

FLOOR FILLERS: Below is a marked out floor waiting to be tiled, together with some pre-assembled groups of tiles... Can you fit them together so that they fill the floor?

Answer on page 186

JIGSAW:
Which four of the pieces below can complete the jigsaw and make a perfect square?

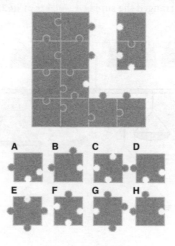

A   B   C   D

E   F   G   H

Answer on page 187

LOGIC SEQUENCE:
The balls below have been rearrange. Can you work out the new sequence of the balls from the clues given below?

The 2 ball isn't touching the 5 or the 4.
The 4 ball is touching the 10 but not the 6.
The 8 ball is immediately to the left of the 6.
The bottom row totals 16.

Answer on page 187

SCALES:
The arms of these scales are divided into sections - a weight two sections away from the middle will be twice as heavy as a weight one section away. Can you arranged the supplied weights in such a way as to balance the whole scale?

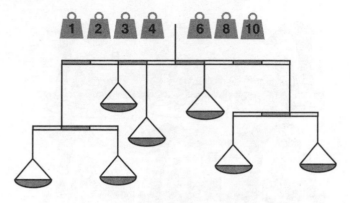

Answer on page 187

NUMBER MOUNTAIN:
Replace the question marks with numbers so that each pair of blocks adds up to the block directly above them.

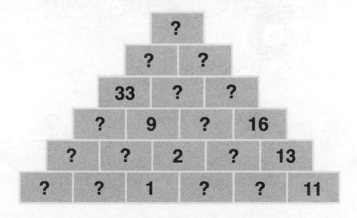

Answer on page 187

MIRROR IMAGE: Only one of these pictures is an exact mirror image of the first one. Can you spot it?

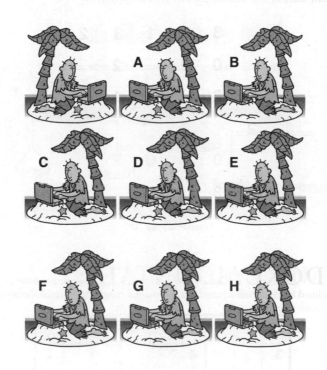

Answer on page 187

LOOPLINK:
Connect adjacent dots with either horizontal or vertical lines to create a continuous unbroken loop which never crosses over itself. Some, but not all of the boxes are numbered. The numbers in these boxes tell you how many sides of that box are used by your unbroken line.

3	2	1	3	2
	0	3		2
2	2		1	1	2
2		3			2
	0	2	0	2
2	3		3		1

Answer on page 187

SUDOKU:
Complete the grid so that all rows and columns, and each outlined block of nine squares, contain the numbers 1, 2, 3, 4, 5, 6, 7, 8 and 9.

	8	1	2	3		5		4
3			4					8
	4	6			5			
	6			2		3		5
1		4						7
			7			9		
		3					8	
7	2			9		1		
			8		3	6		2

Answer on page 187

MATRIX: Which of the four boxed figures completes the set?

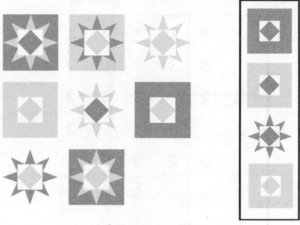

Answer on page 188

THINK OF A NUMBER: Yellowbeard the
pirate had 27 crew under him on his ship, the Blue Goose. He had less prisoners than that in the hold. One night, half of them escaped, leaving the ship exactly 15 percent less occupied than it was before. How many prisoners escaped?

Answer on page 188

KILLER SUDOKU:
Complete the grid so that all rows and columns, and each outlined block of nine squares, contain the numbers 1, 2, 3, 4, 5, 6, 7, 8 and 9. Areas with a dotted outline contain numbers that add up to the total shown.

14			6			17		
17			19	25		11		9
5	13				2		17	
	9			21				9
14		9	14	5	21			
	15			10				20
	4					16	12	
16	7	4	15					
	23					6		

Answer on page 188

HUB SIGNS:
What number should appear in the hub of the second wheel?

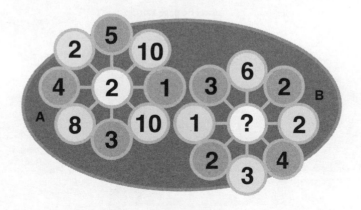

Answer on page 188

SMALL LOGIC:

Jack's garage has seen some fancy cars this week. From the clues below, can you work out when he worked on each car, what colour each was, and what jobs he had to do?

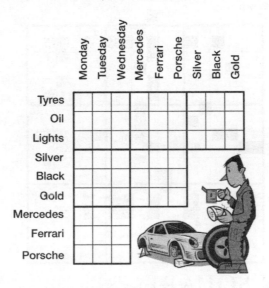

1) The Porsche was black, and didn't need an oil change
2) Jack changed tyres on Monday, but not on the Ferrari
3) The Ferrari was done before the lights but after the silver car

Answer on page 188

SYMMETRY: This picture, when finished, is symmetrical along a vertical line up the middle. Can you shade in the missing squares and work out what the picture is of?

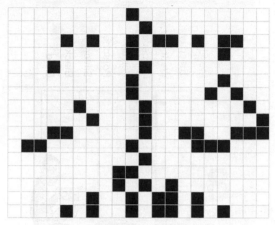

Answer on page 189

LATIN SQUARE: Complete the grid so that every row and column, and every outlined area, contains the letters A, B, C, D, E and F.

				A	
			B		
	C				
				D	
F		E			

Answer on page 189

147

MAGIC SQUARES: Complete the square using nine
consecutive numbers, so that all rows, columns and large diagonals add up to the
same total.

Answer on page 189

REVOLUTIONS: Cog A has 8 teeth, cog B has 9, cog C
has 10 and cog D has 18. How many revolutions must cog A turn through to get
all the cogs into an upright position?

Answer on page 189

148

"Once you finally have the brains, the body is gone or going."

RUBY WAX

MASYU:
Draw a single continuous line around the grid that passes through all the circles. The line must enter and leave each box in the centre of one of its four sides. **Black Circle:** Turn left or right in the box, and the line must pass straight through the next and previous boxes. **White Circle:** Travel straight through the box, and the line must turn in the next and/or previous box.

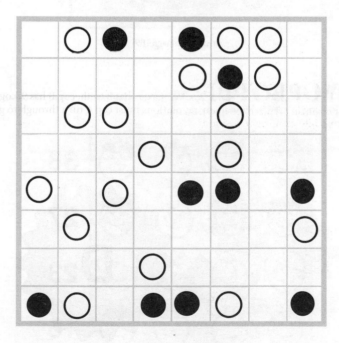

Answer on page 189

ROULETTE:

The roulette ball is dropped into the wheel at the 0 section. When the ball falls into a number 15 seconds later, it has travelled at an average speed of 3 metres per second clockwise, while the wheel has travelled at an average 1 metre per second in the other direction. The ball starts rolling 50 centimetres away from the wheel's centre. Where does it land? Take pi as having a value of exactly 3.2.

Answer on page 189

SUM PEOPLE:

Work out what number is represented by which person and replace the question mark.

Answer on page 190

SHUFFLE: Fill up the shuffle box so that each row, column and long diagonal contains a Jack, Queen, King and Ace of each suit.

Answer on page 190

THE RED CORNER: Use the corners to make the central number the same way in all three cases. What number should replace the question mark?

Answer on page 190

RIDDLE:

At the rocket scientists' canteen, two boffins were chatting in the queue. "How many kids do you have?" asked Professor Numero. "Three" replied Doctor Egghead. "Oh yeah? How old?" said Professor Numero. "Ah," said Dr Egghead, "Well, their ages add up to 13 and multiply to 36, and two of them are twins". "Hmm…" said the Professor. "My eldest is a girl," said Dr Egghead. "Aha! That makes all the difference," said Professor Numero, and promptly told the good Doctor the ages of all his children.

How did that last piece of information help, and how old are the Doctor's kids?

Answer on page 190

152

MINESWEEPER:
The numbers in some squares in the grid indicate the exact number of black squares that should surround it. Shade these squares until all the numbers are surrounded by the correct number of black squares.

	2	1	1		3		2
4		3		1			
				1		1	1
4		4		2		0	
	2	2			3	3	
2		2	4				
	3					6	3
2			3	4		3	

Answer on page 190

MORE OR LESS:
The arrows indicate whether a number in a box is greater or smaller than an adjacent number. Complete the grid so that all rows and columns contain the numbers 1 to 6.

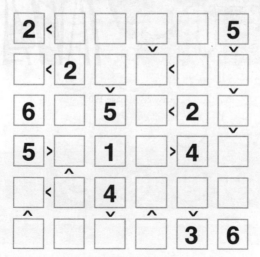

Answer on page 190

153

SIGNPOST: Can you crack the logical secret behind the numbers by these footballers' names, and work out what number Fabregas might be?

Answer on page 191

SUM PEOPLE: Work out what number is represented by which person and replace the question mark.

Answer on page 191

154

SCALES:
The arms of these scales are divided into sections – a weight two sections away from the middle will be twice as heavy as a weight one section away. Can you arrange the supplied weights in such a way as to balance the whole scale?

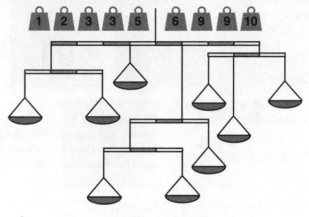

Answer on page 191

SAFECRACKER:
To open the safe, all the buttons must be pressed in the correct order before the "open" button is pressed. What is the first button pressed in your sequence?

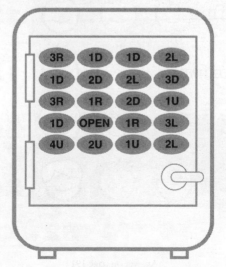

Answer on page 191

155

ANSWERS

Page 7

BITS AND PIECES
Answer: A and G, B and D,
C and H, E and F

BOXES
Solution: A line on the right or
bottom of this square will only give
up one box to your opponent

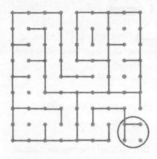

Page 8

CUT AND FOLD
Answer A

GAME OF TWO HALVES
Solution: C and D

Page 9

DOUBLE DRAT

Page 10

IN THE AREA
Answer: 5,000 square millimetres. Each
20 x 20 square represents 400 mm². 12
and a half squares are used

JIGSAW
Answer: A, C and E

Page 11

SUM PEOPLE
Answer 6

1

2

3

4

SHAPE SHIFTING

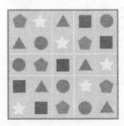

156

Page 12

POTS OF DOTS
Solution: 13

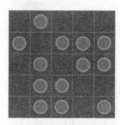

PICTURE PARTS
Answer: A

Page 13

ODD CLOCKS
Answer: 1.55 am on Wednesday in Singapore and 2.55 pm on Tuesday in Buenos Aires

MASYU

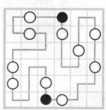

Page 14

MATRIX
Solution:

Each horizontal and vertical line contains a white star, a yellow star and a circled star. Each line contains a green and orange halved circle that has been turned through 0 degrees, 90 degrees and 180 degrees. The missing image should contain a white star, and a circle that has been turned through 90 degrees

FACE IN THE CROWD
Answer: The 5th face down in the third column

Page 15

SUDOKU

8	3	4	1	7	5	2	6	9
1	7	9	2	8	6	4	3	5
2	5	6	9	3	4	1	7	8
4	1	3	8	2	7	5	9	6
7	2	5	3	6	9	8	1	4
9	6	8	4	5	1	7	2	3
6	4	1	7	9	8	3	5	2
3	9	7	5	4	2	6	8	1
5	8	2	6	1	3	9	4	7

RIDDLE

Answer: 7 elephants and 8 emus

Page 16

BITS AND PIECES
Answer: A and F, B and H, C and E, D and G

CUT AND FOLD
Answer: C

Page 17

MIRROR IMAGE
Answer: D

NUMBER JIGSAW

Page 18

MISSING LINK
Answer: A square containing a white circle and a black number 2. Each row and column contains two white circles and numbers that add up to five

PICTURE PARTS
Answer: A

Page 19

SUM PEOPLE
Solution: 10

1

2

3

5

USUAL SUSPECTS
Answer: Officer Lassiter is policeman F

Page 20

WHERE'S THE PAIR?
Answer: F and G are the pair

ODD CLOCKS
Answer: 7.15 am on Saturday in Melbourne
11.15 pm on Friday in Madrid

Page 21

SUM TOTAL
Solution: $21 \times 3 \div 7 - 1 = 8$

WHERE'S THE PAIR?
Answer: D and E are the pair

Page 22

WHERE'S THE PAIR?
Answer: E and I are the pair

Page 23

MAGIC SQUARES
Solution:

4	9	2
3	5	7
8	1	6

DEEP SEA DRESSER
Answer: F, D, H, C, B, E, G, A

Page 24

GAME OF TWO HALVES
Solution: B and F

HUB SIGNS
Answer:
A) 8 – subtract the numbers opposite each other
B) 18 – add the opposite numbers

Page 25

PAINT BY NUMBERS
Solution:

Page 26

RIDDLE
Answer: Six. He ate two on Monday and two more on Tuesday

CATS AND COGS
Answer: Down

Page 27

CHECKERS

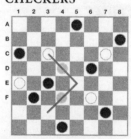

IN THE AREA
Answer: 3400 square millimetres.
Each 20 x 20 square represents
400 mm². 5 squares (2000 mm²) and
7 half-square triangles (1400 mm²)
form the bird

ANSWERS

Page 28

MATRIX

Answer: D. Each horizontal and
vertical line contains two airships
with dark-shaded fins, and one
with light-shaded fins. Each line
contains two airships with dark-
shaded gondolas underneath, and
one with a light-shaded gondola.
Each line contains two airships
facing left and one facing right.
Each line contains two airships
with four lights on the balloon,
and one with three lights.
The missing image has light-
shaded fins, a light-shaded
gondola, faces left and has four
lights on the balloon:

MISSING LINK

Answer: A square containing a dot.
All the rows and columns should
contain two white stars and one dot

Page 29

SUM TOTAL

Solution: 16 + 2 ÷ 3 x 1 = 6

MORE OR LESS

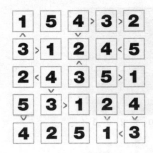

Page 30

RIDDLE

Answer: Just 4.

BOXES

Solution: A line on the top or bottom
of this square will only give up one
box to your opponent

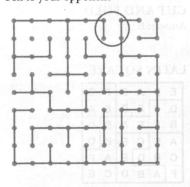

Page 31

DOUBLE DRAT
Answer: 19

BOATS AND BUOYS

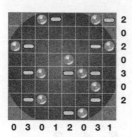

Page 32

RIDDLE
Answer: Tony has 5 bags, Tina has 7

CUBISM
Answer: 3

Page 33

CUT AND FOLD
Answer: B

LATIN SQUARE

Page 34

RIDDLE
Answer: The head and tail are 9 centimetres long, the middle is 27 centimetres long

Page 35

BITS AND PIECES
Answer: A and G, B and H, C and F, D and E

MATRIX
Solution: Each horizontal or vertical line contains a group of 4 black dots, a group of 4 white dots and a single white dot. Each line contains a light grey symbol, a dark grey symbol and a black symbol. The missing picture must be a black symbol with 4 black (and therefore invisible) dots

ANSWERS

Page 36

NEXT!
Answer: D. The colours on the ball are alternating, while the number on it is increasing, by 1, then 2, then 3 etc

NEXT!
Answer: D. The star and circle are swapping places each time. The smallest shape is taking the shade of the previous background square. The background square is taking the shade of the previous medium-sized shape, and the medium-sized shape is taking the shade of the previous smallest shape

Page 37

BLOCK PARTY
Answer: 76

PICTURE PARTS
Answer: C

Page 38

POTS OF DOTS

Solution: 18

SUM TOTAL
Solution: $9 \times 2 \times 3 \div 9 = 6$

Page 39

RIDDLE
Answer: $305 dollars. Three of each denomination and one more $50 bill

BLOCK PARTY
Answer: 24

Page 40

BOXES
Solution: A line on either side of this square will only give up one box to your opponent

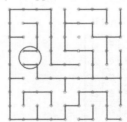

162

DOUBLE DRAT
Answer: A

Page 41

CHECKERS

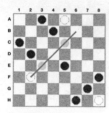

BOXES
Solution: A line on either side of this square will only give up one box to your opponent

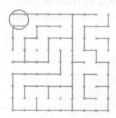

Page 42

DRESSING SNOWMAN
Answer: G, B, F, E, D, H, A, C

Page 43

RIDDLE
Answer: Bread A and B go under the grill. One minute later, Gordon tuns bread A over and swaps bread B for Bread C. One minute later he removes bread A, turns over bread C and puts B back under for a further minute

X AND O

1	2	4	4	3	2
6	X	O	X	X	4
3	X	O	O	X	4
2	O	X	O	O	3
2	O	O	X	O	1
2	3	2	2	5	1

Page 44

IN THE AREA
Answer: 5400 square millimetres. Each 20×20 square represents $400mm^2$. 11 squares ($4400mm^2$) and 5 half-square triangles ($1000mm^2$) form the Q

THINK OF A NUMBER
Answer: 70 percent. Total number of doughnuts - 40, becomes 100 when multiplied by 2.5. Multiply the other numbers by 2.5 to get percentages

ANSWERS

Page 45

MIRROR IMAGE
Answer: B

Page 46

MATRIX

Solution: Each horizontal and vertical line contains 1 circle, 1 square and 1 triangle. Each line contains a yellow star, a white star and one picture without a star. Each line contains an orange symbol, a red symbol and a yellow symbol. The missing picture must be a yellow circle containing a yellow star

SYMMETRY
Solution below

Page 47

NUMBER MOUNTAIN

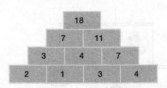

ODD CLOCKS
Answer: 3.30am on Sunday in Karachi, 11.90pm on Saturday in Paris

Page 48

PICTURE PARTS
Answer: B

SUM TOTAL
Solution: $4 \times 8 - 7 \div 5 = 5$

Page 49

PIECE PUZZLE
Answer: B

PICTURE PARTS
Answer: A

Page 50

SCALES

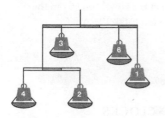

SUM PEOPLE
Solution: 11

Page 52

SUDOKU SIXPACK

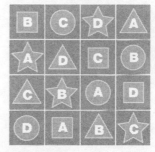

SHUFFLE
Solution: 146

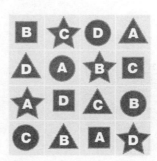

Page 51

PAINT BY NUMBERS
Solution: 2 Chess pieces

Page 53

SHUFFLE

Page 53

SHAPE STACKER
Answer: 48.
The numbers represent the number
of sides in the shape they occupy.
when shapes overlap, the numbers are
multiplied. $3 \times 4 \times 4 = 48$

Page 54

SHAPE SHIFTING

Page 55

RIDDLE
Answer: 4 hamsters and 3 cages

SIGNPOST
Answer: 6. Score three for each
consonant and two for a vowel.
Subtract the vowel total from the
consonant total. 12 - 6 = 6

Page 57

BOXES

CUT AND FOLD
Answer: A

Page 58

MAGIC SQUARES

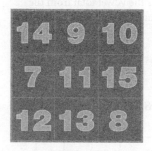

MASYU

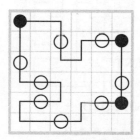

Page 59

RIDDLE

Answer: 10. On the 10th jump he makes it!

THINK OF A NUMBER

Answer: Two thirds and one third.
351 divided by 3 is 117 (39 + 78) 117
× 2 = 234 (203 + 31)

Page 60

THINK OF A NUMBER

Solution: 16

 2

 3

 4

 5

TENTS AND TREES

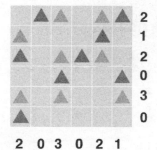

Page 61

SIGNPOST

Answer: 42
Score one for a consonant and two
for a vowel, then multiply the totals
together.
6 × 7 = 42

BLOCK PARTY

Answer: 68

ANSWERS

Page 62

WHERE'S THE PAIR
Answer: B and H are the pair

DOUBLE DRAT

Page 63

MORE OR LESS

2 < 3	1	5 > 4

$$2 < 3 \quad 1 \quad 5 > 4$$
$$5 \quad 1 \quad 4 \quad 3 \quad 2$$
$$4 < 5 \quad 2 \quad 1 \quad 3$$
$$3 > 2 \quad 5 \quad 4 \quad 1$$
$$1 < 4 \quad 3 > 2 \quad 5$$

Page 64

PERCENTAGE POINT
44% is darker, 56% is lighter. 11 out of 25 squares in the grid are darker, 14 are lighter. Multiply both numbers by 4 and you see a percentage

RIDDLE
Answer: Thursday. The goat is lying!

Page 65

BOX IT

BOXES

Page 66

TREE TENT

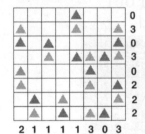

ANSWERS

CHECKERS

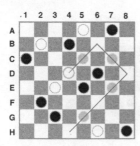

Page 67

DICE PUZZLE
Answer: 4. Subtract the right face from the front face and multiply by the top one

FIGURE IT OUT

Page 68

GAME OF THREE HALVES
Solution:
A, B, and D

LATIN SQUARE

E	C	A	D	F	B
A	B	C	E	D	F
D	F	E	B	C	A
C	D	F	A	B	E
B	E	D	F	A	C
F	A	B	C	E	D

Page 69

LOOPLINK

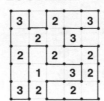

MASYU

Page 70

MORE OR LESS

4	5	3	6 ›	2	1
6 ›	3 ›	2	1	5 ›	4
1	2	6	3	4	5
2	6	4	5	1	3
5	4	1	2 ‹	3 ‹	6
3	1	5	4 ‹	6	2

Page 71

POTS OF DOTS
Solution: 25

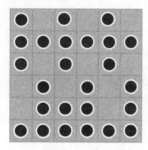

RIDDLE
Answer: The game was on the 24th day of the month

Page 72

SAFECRACKER

SCALES

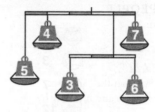

Page 73

SHAPE SHIFTING

SIGNPOST
Answer: 92
Multiply the alphabetical position of the first letter of each city by 5, then subtract the alphabetical position of the last letter 22 x 5 = 110 – 18 = 92

Page 74

SUDOKU SIXPACK

2	6	5	3	1	4
6	4	1	5	3	2
4	1	3	2	5	6
5	2	6	1	4	3
3	5	2	4	6	1
1	3	4	6	2	5

SUM PEOPLE

Solution: 20

1

3

7

12

Page 75

SUDOKU

9	8	2	3	1	7	4	5	6
6	5	1	2	9	4	7	3	8
7	4	3	5	6	8	2	1	9
8	6	7	9	2	1	3	4	5
3	2	5	4	8	6	9	7	1
1	9	4	7	3	5	6	8	2
5	1	9	6	4	3	8	2	7
4	7	6	8	5	2	1	9	3
2	3	8	1	7	9	5	6	4

Page 76

THINK OF A NUMBER

Answer: Kaplutski 56 percent, Wojowitz 44 percent. The total number is 25. Multiply this number, and the others, by 4 to get percentages

VENN DIAGRAMS

Answer: J and D

Page 77

BITS AND PIECES

Answer: Tom Cruise

Page 78

FINDING NEMO

N	O	M	N	M	M	M	M	O	M	M	M
E	N	E	M	N	O	E	E	E	N	N	N
M	E	N	E	E	E	N	O	M	E	E	E
N	M	O	O	O	M	O	E	E	M	M	M
E	N	M	E	M	E	E	N	N	N	N	N
O	E	E	M	E	O	M	E	E	E	M	E
M	O	O	E	M	N	E	O	M	M	N	O
E	M	N	O	E	E	N	E	E	N	M	M
O	E	E	N	O	M	O	N	N	E	E	E
M	N	M	E	M	E	E	M	O	M	O	M
E	E	N	M	E	N	M	E	E	N	M	E
O	O	O	E	M	M	O	N	O	N	O	

MAGIC SQUARES

7	12	11
14	10	6
9	8	13

Page 79

MATRIX

Solution: Each line contains one
target with three holes in the gold,
two holes in the white and one
hole in the red.
Each line contains one target with
three holes in the white, two holes
in the gold and one hole in the red.
Each line contains one target with
three holes in the red, two holes in
the white and one hole in the gold.
The missing picture must have
three holes in the red, two holes in
the white and one in the gold

ODD CLOCKS

Answer:
1.15 pm on Saturday in Miami
6.15 am on Sunday in Auckland

Page 80

RIDDLE
Answer: Monday the 8th

SAFECRACKER

Page 81

LOGIC SEQUENCE

BOXES
Solution: A line on the left or right of
this square will only give up one box
to your opponent

Page 82

X AND O

2	4	5	4	2	7	1
5	X	X	O	X	O	4
4	O	O	X	O	X	3
3	O	X	O	O	X	6
2	O	X	O	O	X	4
5	O	O	O	X	X	5
1	2	4	3	4	6	2

Page 83

PERCENTAGE POINT

Answer: 48% percent is darker, 52% is lighter. 12 out of 25 triangles that make up the shape are darker, 13 are lighter. Multiply both numbers by 4 and you see a percentage

POTS OF DOTS

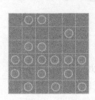

Page 84

CHECKERS

LATIN SQUARE

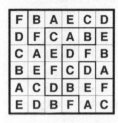

Page 85

NUMBER MOUNTAIN

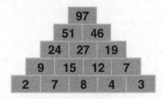

PICTURE PARTS

Answer: B

Page 86

THINK OF A NUMBER
Answer: Bobby. There are 290 sweets in the jar

Page 87

SUM PEOPLE
Solution: 22

 3

 4

 5

 10

THINK OF A NUMBER
Answer: 50.
22 red, 11 yellow and 17 orange

Page 88

SHUFFLE

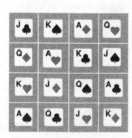

Page 89

DOUBLE DRAT

WHERE'S THE PAIR?
Answer: A and F are the pair

Page 90

THE RED CORNER
Answer: Add the top two corners, then add the bottom two. Then multiply the two totals
$3 + 1 = 4$
$8 + 2 = 10$
$4 \times 10 = 40$

HUB SIGNS
Answers:
A) 24 - multiply the opposite numbers
B) 5 - divide the opposite numbers

Page 91

BOX IT

REVOLUTIONS
Answer: 28 revolutions of
cog A, which will make exactly
35 revolutions of cog B and 20
revolutions of cog C

Page 92

THINK OF A NUMBER
Answer: £100

WHERE'S THE PAIR?
Answer: A and I are the pair

Page 93

CATS AND COGS
Answer: Up

CUT AND FOLD
Answer: C

Page 94

MORE OR LESS

4 > 2	1	3	5	6
2 < 5 > 3	6 > 4	1
3	6	2	4	1	5
6 > 4	5	1	2	3
1	3	4	5 < 6	2
5	1	6	2 < 3	4

RIDDLE
Answer: Stick the signpost back up.
If the sign to Aystown is pointing the
way they have just come, then the
rest of the signs will be pointing the
right way

Page 95

SHAPE SHIFTING

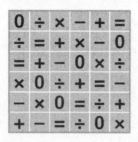

0	÷	×	−	+	=
÷	=	+	×	−	0
=	+	−	0	×	÷
×	0	÷	+	=	−
−	×	0	=	÷	+
+	−	=	÷	0	×

BLOCK PARTY
Answer: 49

Page 96

DOUBLE MAZE

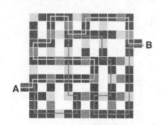

RADAR

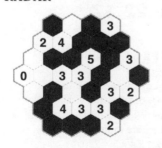

Page 97

SHUFFLE

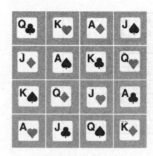

SILHOUETTE
Answer: F

Page 98

SYMBOL SUMS
Answer:
white 1
lightly-shaded 2
dark shaded 3
black 4

IN THE AREA
Answer: 3650 square millimetres.
Each 20×20 square represents
$400\,mm^2$.
4 squares, 6 half–squares,
2 half–square triangles,
3 quarter–squares and
3 8th of a square triangles
are used

Page 99

SUDOKU

5	1	6	7	2	3	4	9	8
4	3	9	1	8	6	2	7	5
2	8	7	9	5	4	6	1	3
6	7	3	2	1	9	5	8	4
1	4	5	6	7	8	9	3	2
9	2	8	3	4	5	1	6	7
3	5	1	8	6	2	7	4	9
7	9	2	4	3	1	8	5	6
8	6	4	5	9	7	3	2	1

Page 100

SUDOKU SIXPACK

2	5	1	6	4	3
4	6	3	2	1	5
6	3	5	4	2	1
3	4	6	1	5	2
1	2	4	5	3	6
5	1	2	3	6	4

FLOOR FILLERS

Page 101

TENTS AND TREES

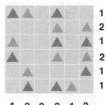

LOOPLINK

3	2	2	2	3
3	1	1	2	2
3	0	2	2	2
3	2	3	2	3
3	1	2	2	2

Page 102

MAGIC SQUARES

23	18	19
16	20	24
21	22	17

SHAPE STACKER

Answer: 720
The numbers represent the
number of sides in the shape they
occupy. When shapes overlap, the
numbers are multiplied
3 x 3 x 4 x 4 x 5 = 720

Page 103

ODD CLOCKS
Answer:
3.25 am on Thursday in Karachi.
5.25 pm on Wednesday in Rio

Page 104

SIGNPOST
Answer: 16
Multiply the alphabetical position of
the first letter of each name by the
number of vowels it contains. H = 8
and Hong Kong contains
2 vowels. 8 x 2 = 16

MIRROR IMAGE
Answer: H

Page 105

NUMBER SWEEP

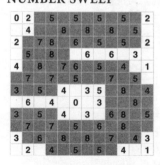

SCALES

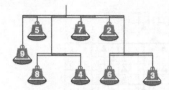

Page 107

MINESWEEPER

WHERE'S THE PAIR?
Answer: B and G are the pair

Page 108

MASYU

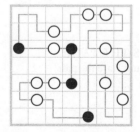

CAMP CONIFER

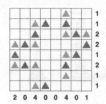

Page 109

CODOKU SIX

$M + 6 = S$ $U + 4 = Y$
$C + 1 = D$ $1 + 5 = N$
$B + 3 = E$ $W + 2 = Y$

Answer: SYDNEY

CUBE VOLUME

Answer: 6272 cubic centimetres. Each little cube measures 4 x 4 x 4 cm, or 64 cubic centimetres, and there are 98 little cubes left. 64 x 98 = 6272

Page 110

WHERE'S THE PAIR?

Answer: B and F are the pair

Page 111

PERCENTAGE POINT

Answer: There are 25 honeycomb cells and 8 bees. Multiply both figures by 4 and we get an occupation percentage of 32%. 6 out of 8 bees, or three-quarters, or 75%, are awake.

MINESWEEPER

Page 112

LOGIC SEQUENCE

A PIECE OF PIE

Answer: 12. The inner numbers are made up of the two outer numbers of the opposite segment multiplied. 4 x 3 = 12

Page 113

FIVE-POINT PROBLEM
Solution: Each pentagon contains numbers that add up to 20, with the sides nearest adjoining pentagons adding up to 10

THE GREAT DIVIDE

Page 114

KILLER SIX

5	1	4	6	2	3
6	4	5	3	1	2
4	2	3	1	6	5
3	6	2	4	5	1
2	3	1	5	4	6
1	5	6	2	3	4

LOOPLINK

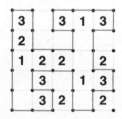

Page 115

MASYU

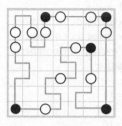

MINI NONOGRAM

Page 116

MIRROR IMAGE
Answer: E

Page 117

SHAPE STACKER
Answer: 2520
The numbers represent the number of sides in the shape they occupy. When shapes overlap, the numbers are added together

A: 6 + 4 + 4 = 14
B: 10 + 4 + 4 = 18
C: 5 + 4 + 1 = 10

14 x 18 x 10 = 2520

SILHOUETTE
Answer: D

Page 118

SUM PEOPLE
Solution: 25

 4

5

 6

 9

Page 119

SUM PEOPLE
Solution: 55

 1

 5

10

 20

WHERE'S THE PAIR?
Answer: C and H are the pair

Page 120

CAN YOU CUT IT?

DICE PUZZLE
Answer: D. The number six is turned 90 degrees compared to the other dice

Page 121

FLOOR FILLERS

HUB SIGNS
Answer: 6. Subtract the total of the numbers in the darker circles from the total of the numbers in the lighter circles in both cases

Page 122

JIGSAW
Answer: A, C, E and F

LATIN SQUARE

B	F	E	A	C	D
F	A	D	C	E	B
D	C	A	B	F	E
A	E	C	D	B	F
C	B	F	E	D	A
E	D	B	F	A	C

Page 123

LOGIC SEQUENCE

MINESWEEPER

Page 124

BATTLESHIPS

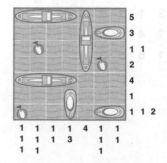

Page 125

CAMP CONIFER

▲	▲				▲	▲		2
	▲			▲				0
	▲		▲		▲	▲	▲	4
		▲						0
								0
				▲	▲	▲		2
▲						▲		1
▲					▲	▲		1

1 2 0 1 1 1 3 1

LOOPLINK

3	1	2	2		3
3		2		2	2
2	2		2		
	3	1	3	3	2
2		2		2	
2	2		2		2

Page 126

MORE OR LESS

1	5	2 < 3	6 > 4
2	6	3	4 < 5	1
6	4	5	1	2 < 3
5 > 3	1	2	4	6
3	2	4 < 6	1	5
4	1	6 > 5	3	2

NUMBER CHUNKS

8	2	1	2	2	4
6	3	1	1	6	3
4	9	9	9	3	5
5	7	1	5	5	5
2	7	3	1	6	4
9	7	3	2	3	7

Page 127

SAFECRACKER

1D	1R	2D	3L
1R	3D	1R	1U
OPEN	2U	1U	2D
1D	2R	2L	1U
2U	1U	1U	1L

SUDOKU

5	2	9	1	6	8	3	4	7
1	3	7	9	2	4	6	8	5
4	6	8	7	3	5	1	9	2
6	7	1	4	5	9	2	3	8
3	9	4	2	8	1	5	7	6
2	8	5	6	7	3	4	1	9
7	1	6	8	4	2	9	5	3
8	4	3	5	9	6	7	2	1
9	5	2	3	1	7	8	6	4

Page 128

CAMP CONIFER

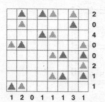

Page 129

CAN YOU CUT IT?

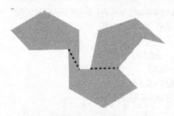

FIVE POINT PROBLEM

Solution: Each pentagon contains numbers that add up to 24, with the sides facing each other on adjoining pentagons, when multiplied together, also making 24

Page 130

GRIDLOCK

Answer: A. Each row and column in the grid contains shapes whose sides total 12, two of which are light and one of which is dark

KILLER SIX

3	1	4	5	2	6
5	6	1	2	3	4
1	5	6	3	4	2
2	4	3	1	6	5
4	3	2	6	5	1
6	2	5	4	1	3

Page 131

HUB SIGNS

Answer: 2. Divide the total of the numbers in the darker circles by the total of the numbers in the lighter circles in each case

LOOPLINK

1		2		2	2
2	2	3	2		3
	0	3	2	2	2
	3			2	
1		2	2	1	2
3	2	2	2		3

Page 132

MAGIC SQUARES

5	10	9
12	8	4
7	6	11

THE GREAT DIVIDE

Page 133

SMALL LOGIC

	Forest	Roadside	Field	Jar	Bottle	Matchbox	Morning	Afternoon	Evening
Beetle			✓				✓		
Spider		✓		✓					✓
Butterfly	✓					✓		✓	
Morning			✓		✓				
Afternoon	✓					✓			
Evening		✓		✓					
Jar		✓							
Bottle			✓						
Matchbox	✓								

SUDOKU

1	2	6	9	7	8	5	3	4
8	4	7	1	3	5	2	9	6
3	5	9	6	4	2	1	7	8
9	6	1	8	5	3	7	4	2
7	3	4	2	1	6	9	8	5
2	8	5	7	9	4	6	1	3
4	1	2	3	6	7	8	5	9
6	7	3	5	8	9	4	2	1
5	9	8	4	2	1	3	6	7

Page 134

SUDOKU

2	8	9	6	4	7	3	1	5
4	5	7	1	8	3	6	2	9
6	3	1	9	5	2	7	8	4
1	9	4	2	3	8	5	6	7
8	7	2	5	9	6	4	3	1
5	6	3	7	1	4	8	9	2
9	1	8	3	7	5	2	4	6
3	2	4	4	6	1	9	7	8
7	4	6	8	2	9	1	5	3

THE RED CORNER

Answer: 36. Add all the red corners
and multiply the total by two. 3 + 3 +
7 + 5 = 18 x 2 = 36

Page 135

CODOKU SIX

Z	K	A	B	Y	J
B	A	Y	J	Z	K
K	Y	B	A	J	Z
Y	J	Z	K	B	A
A	B	J	Z	K	Y
J	Z	K	Y	A	B

2	1	6	4	3	5
1	4	3	2	5	6
3	5	4	6	1	2
4	2	1	5	6	3
5	6	2	1	3	4
6	3	5	4	1	2

B+6=H Z+1=A
K+3=N Y+5=D
A+4=E J+2=L
Answer: HANDEL

NUMBER MOUNTAIN

			216			
		109	107			
	53	56	51			
24	29	27	24			
11	13	16	11	13		
5	6	7	9	2	11	

Page 136

SYMMETRY

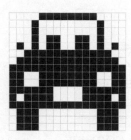

CUBE VOLUME

Answer: 2484 cubic centimetres. Each little cube measures 3 x 3 x 3 cm, or 27 cubic centimetres, and there are 92 little cubes left. 27 x 92 = 2484

Page 137

DICE PUZZLE

Answer: B. The right hand side should be showing a six

KILLER SIX

5	1	6	4	2	3
4	3	1	5	6	2
6	2	5	1	3	4
3	6	4	2	1	5
1	5	2	3	4	6
2	4	3	6	5	1

Page 138

MASYU

MINI NONOGRAM

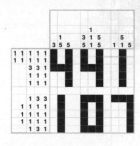

Page 139

NUMBER CHUNKS

FLOOR FILLERS

Page 140

JIGSAW
Answer: A, C, E and H

LOGIC SEQUENCE

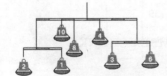

Page 141

SCALES

NUMBER MOUNTAIN

				82				
			47		35			
		33		14		21		
	24		9		5		16	
17		7		2		3		13
11	6		1		1		2	11

Page 142

MIRROR IMAGE
Answer: D

Page 143

LOOPLINK

2	3	2	1	3	2
3	0	3	1	2	2
2	2	2	1	1	2
2	2	3	3	3	2
3	0	2	0	2	2
2	3	3	3	2	1

SUDOKU

9	8	1	2	3	7	5	6	4
3	7	5	4	6	1	2	9	8
2	4	6	9	8	5	7	3	1
8	6	7	1	2	9	3	4	5
1	9	4	3	5	6	8	2	7
5	3	2	7	4	8	9	1	6
6	1	3	5	7	2	4	8	9
7	2	8	6	9	4	1	5	3
4	5	9	8	1	3	6	7	2

Page 144

MATRIX

Every vertical and horizontal line contains one darker, one lighter and one white outer box. Each line also contains one darker inner diamond and two lighter ones. Finally each line contains one darker star and two lighter ones. The missing image should be a lighter outer box with a darker inner diamond and a lighter star.

THINK OF A NUMBER

Solution: 6. There were 12 prisoners in the hold before the escape, making 40 people in all on the ship, and 15 percent of 40 is 6

Page 145

KILLER SUDOKU

2	9	3	5	1	8	4	6	7
8	4	5	3	6	7	2	9	1
1	7	6	9	4	2	3	5	8
4	6	2	7	8	9	1	3	5
3	1	9	2	5	6	8	7	4
5	8	7	4	3	1	6	2	9
6	3	1	8	7	5	9	4	2
9	5	4	1	2	3	7	8	6
7	2	8	6	9	4	5	1	3

HUB SIGNS

Answer: 4. Multiply all the numbers in darker circles and add all the numbers in lighter circles. Divide the darker total by the lighter one.
3 x 2 x 4 x 2 = 48
1 + 6 + 2 + 3 = 12
48 divided by 12 is 4

Page 146

SMALL LOGIC

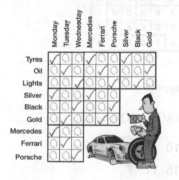

IN THE AREA

Answer: 2550 square millimetres. Each 20 x 20 square represents 400 mm². 4 squares, 4 half-square triangles and 2 half-squares make up the tree. Minus 250mm² that make up the oranges

Page 147

SYMMETRY

LATIN SQUARE

B	F	C	D	A	E
D	A	F	B	E	C
E	C	A	F	B	D
A	E	B	C	D	F
F	D	E	A	C	B
C	B	D	E	F	A

Page 148

MAGIC SQUARES

10	9	14
15	11	7
8	13	12

REVOLUTIONS

Answer: 22 and a half revolutions of cog A, which will make exactly 20 revolutions of cog B, 18 revolutions of cog C and 10 revolutions of cog D

Page 149

MASYU

Page 480

Page 150

ROULETTE

Answer: In the number 6 space. The ball travels at a speed of 4 metres per second (relative to the wheel) for 15 seconds, making a distance of 6000 centimetres in a clockwise direction. The circumference of the wheel is 320 centimetres (2 x pi (3.2) x radius (50cm)). The ball must then travel 18.75 laps of the wheel, placing it three quarters of the way around the wheel in a clockwise direction, in the 6 space

Page 150

SUM PEOPLE:
Solution: 27

 2

 4

 6

 13

Page 151

SHUFFLE

K♦	J♥	Q♣	A♠
A♠	Q♣	J♦	K♥
J♣	K♠	A♥	Q♦
Q♥	A♦	K♣	J♠

THE RED CORNER
Answer: 50. Multiply the two largest
red corners, then multiply the two
smallest corners. Subtract the smaller
total from the larger.
8 x 7 = 56
6 x 1 = 6
56 − 6 = 50

Page 152

RIDDLE
Answer: 9, 2 and 2. Before he knew
that the twins were younger than the
single child, the Professor could have
come up with the answer 6, 6 and 1

Page 153

MINESWEEPER

MORE OR LESS

2	<	6	3		4		1		5
1	<	2		6	3	<	5		4

2 < 6   3   4   1   5
1 < 2   6   3 < 5   4
6   4   5   1 < 2   3
5 > 3   1   6 > 4   2
3 < 5   4   2   6   1
4   1   2   5   3   6

Page 154

SIGNPOST
Answer: 66. Score one for a
consonant and two for a vowel, then
multiply the total by the alphabetical
position of the first letter. 5 + 6 = 11,
11 x 6 = 66

SUM PEOPLE
Answer: 18

 3

 1

 5

 11

Page 155

SCALES

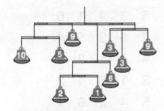

SAFECRACKER

"People say that age is just a state of mind. I say it's more about the state of your body."

GEOFFREY PARFITT